easy to make!
Cakes & Bakes

Good Housekeeping

easy to make!
Cakes & Bakes

COLLINS & BROWN

First published in Great Britain in 2008
by Collins & Brown
10 Southcombe Street
London W14 0RA

An imprint of Anova Books Company Ltd

The Good Housekeeping website is
www.goodhousekeeping.co.uk

1 2 3 4 5 6 7 8 9

ISBN 978-1-84340-441-5

A catalogue record for this book is available from the British
Library.

Reproduction by Dot Gradations Ltd
Printed and bound by SNP Leefung, China

This book can be ordered direct from the publisher. Contact the
marketing department, but try your bookshop first.

www.anovabooks.com

NOTES

- Both metric and imperial measures are given for the
  recipes. Follow either set of measures, not a mixture
  of both, as they are not interchangeable.
- All spoon measures are level.
  1 tsp = 5ml spoon; 1 tbsp = 15ml spoon.
- Ovens and grills must be preheated to the specified
  temperature.
- Use sea salt and freshly ground black pepper unless
  otherwise suggested.
- Fresh herbs should be used unless dried herbs are
  specified in a recipe.
- Medium eggs should be used except where
  otherwise specified. Free-range eggs are
  recommended.
- Note that certain recipes, including mayonnaise,
  lemon curd and some cold desserts, contain raw or
  lightly cooked eggs. The young, elderly, pregnant
  women and anyone with an immune-deficiency
  disease should avoid these, because of the slight risk
  of salmonella.
- Calorie, fat and carbohydrate counts per serving are
  provided for the recipes.

Picture Credits
Photographers: Nicki Dowey; Craig Robertson (all Basics
photography)
Stylist: Helen Trent
Home economist: Lucy McKelvie

Contents

Foreword

Whether it's a well-deserved slice of teabread with a cup of tea after a bracing country walk, (almost) too-pretty-to-eat fairy cakes covered in pastel icing for an afternoon treat, or a many-layered gateau on a special occasion, cakes rightly hold a place at the centre of everything worth celebrating.

There's something magical about cake-making. Flour, sugar, eggs and butter somehow amount to more than the sum of their parts, transforming themselves into mouth-watering treats. Whether you're a novice baker with an hour to spare or an accomplished cook whose idea of perfection is whiling away an afternoon in the kitchen, there's a cake or bake for everyone.

To inspire you, we've gathered together some of our favourite recipes, ranging from melt-in-the-mouth cookies to crisp biscotti, dainty cupcakes to moist fruit loaves and classic sponges. There's also all the information you need to get started – choosing equipment, lining cake tins, basic mixtures, testing and troubleshooting – and for experienced cooks there are tips for perfect baking and decorating cakes and cookies.

In this book you'll find a tempting collection of 101 ideas for cakes and bakes. All the recipes have been triple-tested in the Good Housekeeping kitchens to make sure they work every time. So put on your apron and become a domestic goddess for the day.

Emma

Emma Marsden
Cookery Editor
Good Housekeeping

0

The Basics

Getting started

You don't need much specialist equipment for making cakes and cookies; in fact, you probably have many of these items in your kitchen already.

Weighing and measuring

Scales

Accurate measurement is essential when baking. The most accurate scale is the electronic type, capable of weighing up to 2kg (4½lb) or 5kg (11lb) in increments of 1–5g. Buy one with a flat platform on which you can put your own bowl or measuring jug, and always remember to set the scale to zero before adding the ingredients.

Measuring jugs

These can be plastic or glass, and are available in sizes ranging from 500ml (18fl oz) to 2 litres (3½ pints), or even 3 litres (5¼ pints). Have two – a large one and a small one – marked with both metric and imperial measurements.

Measuring cups

Commonly used in the US, these are used for measuring liquid and dry ingredients. Cups are bought in sets of ¼, ⅓, ½ and 1 cups. A standard 1 cup measure is equivalent to about 250ml (9fl oz).

Measuring spoons

Useful for the smallest units, accurate spoon measurements go from 1.25ml (¼ tsp) to 15ml (1 tbsp).

Mixing

Bowls

For mixing large quantities, such as cake mixtures, you will need at least two large bowls, including one with a diameter of up to 38cm (15in).

- Plastic or glass bowls are best if you need to use them in the microwave.
- Steel bowls with a rubber foot will keep their grip on the worksurface.
- Bowls with gently tapered sides – much wider at the rim than at the base – are useful for mixing dough.

Spoons

For general mixing, the cheap and sturdy wooden spoon still can't be beaten, but equivalents made from thermoplastic materials are heatproof and may suit you better. A large metal spoon for folding ingredients together is also invaluable when baking.

Bakeware

As well as being thin enough to conduct heat quickly and efficiently, bakeware should be sturdy enough not to warp when heated. Most bakeware is made from aluminium, and it may have enamel or non-stick coatings.

Cake tins Available in many shapes and sizes, tins may be single-piece, loose-based or springform.
Loaf tins Available in various sizes, one of the most useful is a 900g (2lb) tin.
Pie tins and muffin tins You should have both single-piece tins and loose-based tins for flans and pies.
Oven-safe silicone is safe to touch straight from the oven, is inherently non-stick and is also flexible – making it easy to remove muffins and other bakes.

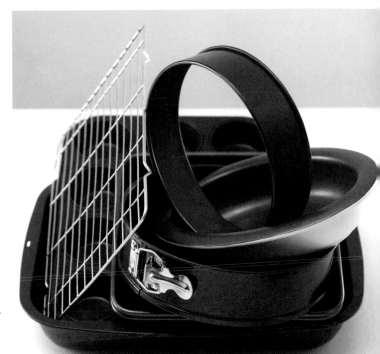

Electrical equipment

Food processor For certain tasks, such as making breadcrumbs or pastry or for chopping large quantities of nuts, food processors are unbeatable. Most come with a number of attachments – dough hooks, graters, slicers – which are worth having, even if only for occasional use.
Blender These are less versatile than food processors, but unmatched for certain tasks, such as puréeing fruit. The traditional jug blender is great but some cooks prefer a hand-held stick blender, which can be used directly in a pan, bowl or jug.
Freestanding mixer An electric mixer may be a good investment if you do a lot of baking, but decide first whether you have space in your kitchen. They are big and heavy to store.
Electric hand mixer Useful for creaming together butter and sugar in baking and for making meringues. They don't take up a lot of space and can be packed away easily.

Other useful utensils

Baking sheets (two)	Cooling racks (two)
Spatulas	Palette knife
Wire whisks	Ruler
Fine sieve	Dredger
Microplane grater	Serrated knife
Rolling pin	Icing bag and piping
Thin skewers	nozzles
Cookie cutters	Vegetable peeler

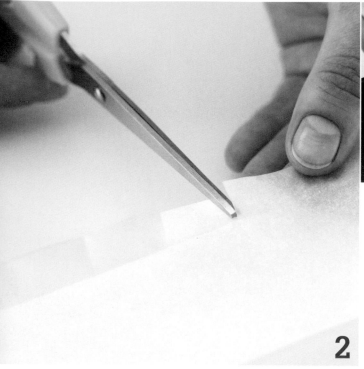

2

Lining tins

When making cakes, you usually need to grease and/or line the tin with greaseproof paper before filling it with cake mixture. Lightly grease the tin first to help keep the paper in place. You will need to use different techniques according to the shape of the tin.

Round tin

1 Put the tin on a sheet of greaseproof paper and draw a circle around its circumference. Cut out the circle just inside the drawn line.

2 Cut a strip or strips about 2cm (³/₄ in) wider than the depth of the tin and fold up one long edge of each strip by 1cm (¹/₂in). Make cuts, about 2.5cm (1in) apart, through the folded edge of the strip(s) up to the fold line.

3 Lightly grease the tin with butter, making sure it is completely coated.

4 Press the strip(s) on to the sides of the tin so that the snipped edge sits on the base.

5 Lay the circle in the bottom of the tin and grease the paper.

Swiss roll tin

Use this method for Swiss roll or other shallow baking tins.

1 Lightly grease the tin with butter, making sure it is completely coated.

2 Cut a piece of baking parchment into a rectangle 7.5cm (3in) wider and longer than the tin. Press it into the tin and cut at the corners, then fold to fit neatly. Grease all over.

2

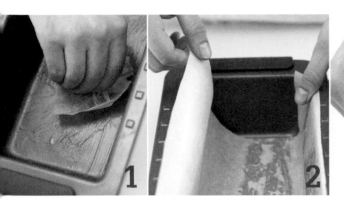

Loaf tin

1 Lightly grease the tin with butter, making sure it is completely coated.

2 Cut out a sheet of greaseproof paper to the same length as the base and wide enough to cover both the base and the long sides. Press it into position, making sure that it sits snugly in the corners.

3 Now cut another sheet to the same width as the base and long enough to cover both the base and the ends of the tin. Press into place. Grease the paper all over.

3

Perfect lining

Use greaseproof paper for all cakes and baking parchment for roulades and meringues.
Apply the butter with a small piece of greaseproof paper.
Don't grease too thickly – this 'fries' the edges of the cake.

Square tin

1 Cut out a square of greaseproof paper slightly smaller than the base of the tin. Cut four strips about 2cm (³/₄in) wider than the depth of the tin and fold up one of the longest edges of each strip by 1cm (¹/₂in).

2 Lightly grease the tin with butter, making sure it is coated on all sides and in the corners.

3 Cut one strip to the length of the side of the tin and press into place in one corner then along the length of the strip with the narrow folded section sitting on the base. Continue, cutting to fit into the corners, to cover all four sides.

4 Lay the square on the base of the tin, then grease the paper, taking care not to move the side strips.

Preparing eggs

Mastering three simple techniques – cracking, separating and whisking – will make every aspect of baking easier.

Cracking and separating

You'll need to separate eggs for making meringues and some cakes. It's easy, but it requires care. If you're separating more than one egg, break each one into an individual cup. Separating them individually means that if you break one yolk, you won't spoil the whole batch. Keeping the whites yolk-free is particularly important for techniques such as whisking.

1 Crack the egg more carefully than usual: right in the middle to make a break between the two halves that is just wide enough to get your thumbnail into.

2 Holding the egg over a bowl with the large end pointing down, carefully lift off the small half. Some of the white will drip and slide into the bowl while the yolk sits in the large end of the shell.

3 Carefully slide the yolk into the smaller end, then back into the large end to allow the remaining white to drop into the bowl. Take care not to break the yolk; even a speck can stop the whites from whisking up.

How can I tell if my eggs are fresh?

A fresh egg should feel heavy in your hand and will sink to the bottom of the bowl or float on its side when put into water (1).
Older eggs, over two weeks old, will float vertically (2).

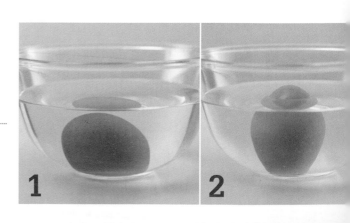

Whisking

1 Use an electric mixer or wire whisk. Make sure that there is no trace of yolk in the whites and that the whisk and bowl are clean and dry. At a low speed, use the whisk in a small area of the whites until it starts to become foamy.

2 Increase the speed and work the whisk through the whites until glossy and soft rounded peaks form. Do not over-whisk as the foam will become dry and grainy.

Meringues

Baking meringues is best done whenever you know you won't be needing your oven for a good few hours, as they must be left to dry in the turned-off oven for several hours.

To make 12 meringues, you will need:
3 medium egg whites, 175g (6oz) caster sugar.

1 Preheat the oven to 170°C (150°C fan oven) mark 3. Cover a baking sheet with baking parchment. Put the egg whites into a large, clean, grease-free bowl.

2 Whisk them until soft peaks form. Add a spoonful of sugar and whisk until glossy.

3 Keep adding the sugar a spoonful at a time, whisking thoroughly after each addition until you have used half the sugar. The mixture should be thick and glossy.

4 Sprinkle the remaining sugar over the mixture and then gently fold in using a metal spoon.

5 Hold a dessertspoon in each hand and pick up a spoonful of mixture in one spoon, then scrape the other one against it to lift the mixture off. Repeat the process a few times, to form a rough oval shape. Using the empty spoon, push the oval on to the baking sheet; hold it just over the sheet so that it doesn't drop from a great height. Continue this process with the remaining mixture to make 12 meringues.

6 Put the meringues in the oven and bake for 15 minutes, then turn the oven off and leave them in the oven to dry out for several hours or overnight.

Creaming

A classic creamed (Victoria) sponge can be used to make many cakes, including chocolate or fruit.

1   Put the butter and sugar in a bowl and beat with an electric whisk or wooden spoon until pale, soft and creamy.

2   Beat the eggs and gradually add to the butter and sugar mixture, beating well until the mixture is thick and of dropping consistency. If you like, add a spoonful of flour while adding the eggs to prevent curdling.

3   Gently fold in the flour using a large metal spoon or spatula, then spoon the mixture into the prepared tin(s), level the surface and bake.

Making cakes

Many of the cakes and bakes in this book use one of these basic techniques: creaming, whisking, all-in-one.

Whisking

1   Melt the butter in a small pan. Put the eggs and sugar in a large bowl set over a pan of simmering water. Whisk for about 5 minutes with an electric hand mixer until creamy and pale and the mixture leaves a trail when you lift the whisk.

2   Gently fold half the flour into the mixture. Pour the butter around the edge of the mixture, then fold in the remaining flour and butter. Pour into the prepared tin(s) and bake.

All-in-one

1 Put the butter, sugar, eggs, flour and baking powder in a large bowl or mixer.

2 Using an electric hand mixer, mix slowly to start, then increase the speed slightly until well combined. Fold in any remaining ingredients, such as milk or fruit, then spoon into the prepared tin(s) and bake.

Testing fruit cakes

1 To test if a fruit cake is cooked, insert a skewer into the centre of the cake, leave for a few moments, then pull it out. If it comes away clean, the cake is ready.

2 If any mixture sticks to the skewer, the cake is not quite done, so put the cake back in the oven for a few more minutes, then test again with a clean skewer.

Testing sponges

1 Gently press the centre of the sponge. It should feel springy. If it's a whisked cake, it should be just shrinking away from the sides of the tin.

2 If you have to put it back into the oven, close the door gently so that the vibrations don't cause the cake to sink in the centre.

Troubleshooting: fruit cakes

A dense texture may be due to too little raising agent, or adding the eggs too quickly.
A peaked, cracked top may form if the oven is too hot or the cake is too near the top of the oven; the tin is too small; or too much raising agent was used.

Cooling cakes

Sponge cakes should be taken out of their tins soon after baking. Invert on to a wire rack covered with sugar-dusted baking parchment.
Leave fruit cakes to cool in the tin for 15 minutes before turning out.
Allow rich fruit cakes to cool completely before turning out; there is a risk of breaking otherwise.

Making biscuits and cookies

Home-made biscuits are always welcome; the only drawback is they are so moreish – you'll need all your willpower to stay away from the biscuit tin.

Cookie troubleshooting

Although very simple in their composition, biscuits can be surprisingly prone to baking problems because they cook so quickly. It's as well to be aware of the possible problems and to know what can cause them. Following a few key points should minimise most of the risks and potential pitfalls.

Use a shiny-based baking sheet; a darker-coloured sheet will absorb a greater amount of heat and can therefore burn the undersides of the biscuits.

Don't overcrowd the biscuits on the baking sheet or in the oven – air needs to circulate all around them. If you are baking more than one sheet, make sure they are on shelves at least 20.5cm (8in) apart.

Turn the baking sheet(s) around once or twice during baking. Most ovens get hotter in some places than in others, and this can cause uneven cooking.

If you are cooking more than one sheet, be prepared to have them bake at different speeds. Watch them closely for uneven cooking.

Start testing biscuits slightly before you expect them to be cooked. And watch them very closely during the final minutes, as they can go from perfect to overcooked in a matter of only a few seconds.

Like cakes, biscuits must be transferred to a wire rack while they are still hot. The hot baking sheet will continue to cook them, and steam will build up underneath, which can make the bases soggy. As soon as they are cooked, lift the biscuits from the baking sheet and transfer to a wire rack to cool. Some biscuits, however (particularly those made with syrup), need to be left on the baking sheet to firm up a little before they are transferred to a rack.

Ideally, cool the biscuits on a fairly fine-meshed rack.

If possible, raise the rack by putting it on supports so that it is at least a few centimetres higher than the worksurface underneath: the more air circulating underneath, the crisper the bases will be.

If the biscuits are tough or dry, the dough may have been overworked or too much flour may have been added.

Biscuits that spread too much during baking contain too much butter or sugar, or the mixture may have been overbeaten.

A cake-like texture indicates that too much flour was used or the biscuits were baked at too high a temperature.

Rolled Vanilla Biscuits

The easiest way to make biscuits of consistent thickness is by rolling and then cutting using a biscuit cutter. The dough must be firm enough to roll to a thickness of 3mm (1/8in).

To make 48 biscuits, you will need:

175g (6oz) softened unsalted butter, 200g (7oz) golden caster sugar, 350g (12oz) plain flour, 1 medium egg, 2 tsp vanilla bean paste, 2 tbsp golden icing sugar.

1 Preheat the oven to 200°C (180°C fan oven) mark 6. Put the butter, caster sugar, flour, egg and vanilla seeds or extract into a food processor and whiz to combine. Alternatively, cream the butter and sugar, and then stir in the flour, egg and vanilla.

2 Put the dough on a large sheet of baking parchment. Press the dough gently but firmly with the palm of your hand to flatten it slightly, then put another sheet of baking parchment on top – this will prevent the dough from sticking.

3 Use a rolling pin to roll out the dough to 3mm (1/8in) thick, and then remove the top sheet of baking parchment.

4 Using 6.5cm (2 1/2in) cutters, stamp out biscuits, leaving a 3mm (1/8in) gap between each one.

5 Peel off the trimmings around the shapes, then slide the baking parchment and biscuits on to a flat baking sheet.

6 Re-roll the trimmings between two new sheets of baking parchment, then stamp out shapes as before and slide on to another baking sheet.

7 Bake the biscuits for 10–12 minutes until pale golden. Cool for a few minutes, then transfer to a wire rack to cool completely.

8 Dust the biscuits with sifted icing sugar. Store in an airtight container for up to five days.

Shaving

This is the easiest decoration of all because it doesn't call for melting the chocolate.

1 Hold a chocolate bar upright on the worksurface and shave pieces off the edge with a swivel peeler.

2 Alternatively, grate the chocolate, against a coarse or medium-coarse grater, to make very fine shavings.

Using chocolate

As well as being a delicious ingredient in many cakes and bakes, chocolate can be used to make stunning decorations.

Cook's Tip

When melting chocolate, always use a gentle heat.
Make sure the base of the bowl is not touching the water.
However tempting, only stir the chocolate once or twice until it has melted: overstirring will make it thicken into a sticky mess.
Don't let water or steam touch the chocolate or it will 'seize' – become hard and unworkable. If it has siezed, you can try saving it by stirring in a few drops of flavourless vegetable oil.

Melting

For cooking or making decorations, chocolate is usually melted first.

1 Break the chocolate into pieces and put in a heatproof bowl or in the top of a double boiler. Set over a pan of gently simmering water.

2 Heat very gently until the chocolate starts to melt, then stir only once or twice until completely melted.

Chocolate curls

1 Melt the chocolate, as above, and spread it out in a thin layer on a marble slab or clean worksurface. Leave to firm up.

2 Use a sharp blade (such as a pastry scraper, a cook's knife or a very stiff spatula) to scrape through the chocolate at a 45 degree angle. The size of the curls will be determined by the width of the blade.

Chocolate leaves

1 Wash and dry some rose or bay leaves. Spread slightly cooled melted chocolate in a thin, even layer over the shiny side of the leaf. Spread it right out to the edge using a paintbrush, but wipe off any chocolate that drips over the edge.

2 Leave to cool completely. Then, working very gently and carefully, peel the leaf off the chocolate.

Which chocolate to choose?

The type of chocolate you choose will have a dramatic effect on the end product. For the best results, buy chocolate that has a high proportion of cocoa solids, preferably at least 70%. Most supermarkets stock a selection. At the top end of the scale, couverture chocolate is preferred by chefs for confectionery work and gives an intense chocolate flavour; it is probably best reserved for special mousses and gâteaux. It is available in milk, plain and white varieties from specialist chocolate shops.

Blanching and skinning

After nuts have been shelled, they are still coated with a skin, which, although edible, tastes bitter. This is easier to remove if the nuts are blanched or toasted.

1 **Blanching** Put the shelled nuts in a bowl and cover with boiling water. Leave for 2 minutes, then drain.

2 Remove the skins by rubbing the nuts in a teatowel or squeezing between your thumb and index finger.

3 **Toasting** This also improves the flavour. Preheat the oven to 200°C (180°C fan oven) mark 6. Put the shelled nuts on a baking sheet in a single layer, and bake for 8–15 minutes until the skins are lightly coloured. Remove the skins by rubbing the nuts in a teatowel.

Using nuts

Nuts are used in many cakes and cookies. Some can be bought ready-prepared, but there are various tips and techniques that may be helpful.

Chopping

Unless you want very large pieces, the easiest way to chop nuts is in the food processor. Alternatively, place a chopping board on a folded teatowel on the worksurface and use a cook's knife. Only chop about 75g (3oz) of nuts at a time.

1 Put the nuts in a food processor and pulse at 10-second intervals.

2 Chop to the size of coarse breadcrumbs. Store in an airtight container for up to two weeks.
Note: Allow nuts to cool completely after skinning and before chopping.

Storing nuts

Because of their high fat content, nuts do not keep particularly well and turn rancid if kept for too long.
Always buy nuts from a shop with a high turnover of stock so you know they're likely to be fresh.
Store in an airtight container in a cool, dark place, or in the refrigerator, and use well within the 'best before' date on the pack.

Slicing and slivering

Although you can buy sliced and slivered nuts, it's easy enough to make your own.

1 **To slice,** put the nuts on a board. Using a cook's knife, carefully slice the nuts as thinly as required.

2 **To make slivers**, carefully cut the slices to make narrow matchsticks.

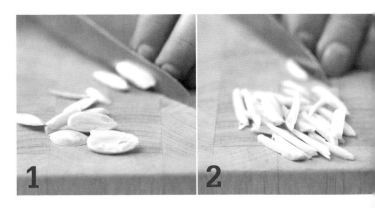

3

4

2

Splitting and filling a cake

1 Allow the cake to cool completely before splitting.

2 Use a knife with a shallow thin blade such as a ham knife, a bread knife or a carving knife. Cut a notch from top to bottom on one side so you will know where to line the pieces up. Cut midway between top and bottom, about 30 per cent of the way through the cake. Turn the cake while cutting, taking care to keep the blade parallel with the base, until you have cut all the way around.

3 Continue cutting until you have cut through the central core; then carefully lift off the top of the cake.

4 Warm the filling slightly to make it easier to spread, then spread over the base, stopping 1cm ($^1/_2$in) from the edge.

5 Carefully place the top layer of cake on top of the filling and gently pat into place.

Finishing touches

Sponge cakes are often made in two tins, but can also be made in a deeper tin, then split and filled with jam, buttercream, cream or mascarpone with sliced fruit.

Decorating cakes and cookies

Drizzling with icing or melted chocolate makes a simple but stylish decoration. Place a sheet of greaseproof paper under a wire rack to catch drips, and leave the cakes to cool completely on the rack. Melt some chocolate (see page 21) or mix 125g (4oz) icing sugar with a little water, lemon or orange juice until it is smooth. Using a teaspoon, drizzle thin trails of icing or chocolate over the cakes and leave to set.

Buttercream Icing

To cover the top of a 20.5cm (8in) cake, you will need:
75g (3oz) unsalted butter, 175g (6oz) icing sugar, sifted, a few drops of vanilla extract, 1–2 tbsp milk.

1 Soften the butter in a mixing bowl, then beat until light and fluffy.

2 Gradually stir in the remaining ingredients and beat until smooth.

Variations

Citrus Replace the vanilla with a little orange, lemon or lime zest, and use some of the fruit's juice in place of the milk.
Chocolate Blend 1 tbsp cocoa powder with 2 tbsp boiling water. Cool, then add to the mixture in place of the milk.

Decorating with fruit

Fresh seasonal fruit make an attractive decoration, either singly or arranged with other fruit. In summer, berries such as strawberries, raspberries and blueberries make an excellent choice. Slice or halve strawberries if you like. You can also use chopped mango and whole redcurrants or sliced kiwi fruit and halved seedless grapes or orange segments.

Using fruit

Citrus fruit is an important flavouring: the grated zest and juice of oranges and lemons are used in many cake mixtures and icings. Other fruit may be used as an ingredient or a colourful, fresh-tasting decoration.

Zesting

Most citrus fruit is sprayed with wax and fungicides or pesticides. Unless you buy unwaxed fruit, wash it with a tiny drop of washing-up liquid and warm water, then rinse with clean water and dry thoroughly on kitchen paper.
To use a grater, rub the fruit over the grater, using a medium pressure to remove the zest without removing the white pith.
To use a zester, press the blade into the citrus skin and run it along the surface to take off long shreds.

Slicing apples

Core and peel the apple, then cut in half.
For flat slices, hold the apple cut side down and slice with the knife blade at right angles to the hollow left by the core.
For crescent-shaped slices, stand the fruit on its end and cut slices into the hollow as if you were slicing a pie.

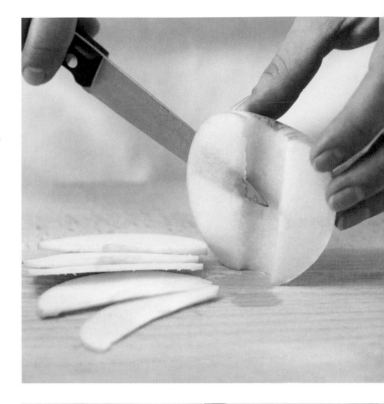

Segmenting citrus fruits

1 Cut off a slice at both ends of the fruit, then cut off the peel, just inside the white pith.

2 Hold fruit over a bowl to catch the juice and cut between the segments just inside the membrane to release the flesh. Continue until all the segments are removed. Squeeze the juice from the membrane into the bowl and use as required.

Hulling strawberries

1 Wash the strawberries gently and dry on kitchen paper.

2 Remove the hull (the centre part that was attached to the plant) from the strawberry using a strawberry huller or a small sharp knife. Put the knife into the small, hard area beneath the green stalk and gently rotate to remove a small, cone-shaped piece.

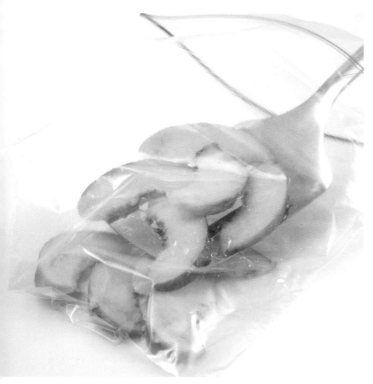

Food storage and hygiene

Storing food properly and preparing food in a hygienic way is important to ensure that food remains as nutritious and flavourful as possible, and to reduce the risk of food poisoning.

Hygiene

When you are preparing food, always follow these important guidelines:

Wash your hands thoroughly before handling food and again between handling different types of food, such as raw and cooked meat and poultry. If you have any cuts or grazes on your hands, be sure to keep them covered with a waterproof plaster.

Wash down worksurfaces regularly with a mild detergent solution or multi-surface cleaner.

Use a dishwasher if available. Otherwise, wear rubber gloves for washing-up, so that the water temperature can be hotter than unprotected hands can bear. Change drying-up cloths and cleaning cloths regularly. Note that leaving dishes to drain is more hygienic than drying them with a teatowel.

Keep pets out of the kitchen if possible; or make sure they stay away from worksurfaces. Never allow animals on to worksurfaces.

Shopping

Always choose fresh ingredients in prime condition from stores and markets that have a regular turnover of stock to ensure you buy the freshest produce possible.

Make sure items are within their 'best before' or 'use by' date. (Foods with a longer shelf life have a 'best before' date; more perishable items have a 'use by' date.)

Pack frozen and chilled items in an insulated cool bag at the check-out and put them into the freezer or refrigerator as soon as you get home.

During warm weather in particular, buy perishable foods just before you return home. When packing items at the check-out, sort them according to where you will store them when you get home – the refrigerator, freezer, storecupboard, vegetable rack, fruit bowl, etc. This will make unpacking easier – and quicker.

The storecupboard

Although storecupboard ingredients will generally last a long time, correct storage is important:

Always check packaging for storage advice – even with familiar foods, because storage requirements may change if additives, sugar or salt have been reduced.

Check storecupboard foods for their 'best before' or 'use by' date and do not use them if the date has passed.

Keep all food cupboards scrupulously clean and make sure food containers and packets are properly sealed.

Once opened, treat canned foods as though fresh. Always transfer the contents to a clean container, cover and keep in the refrigerator. Similarly, jars, sauce bottles and cartons should be kept chilled after opening. (Check the label for safe storage times after opening.)

Transfer dry goods such as sugar, rice and pasta to moisture-proof containers. When supplies are used up, wash the container well and thoroughly dry before refilling with new supplies.

Store oils in a dark cupboard away from any heat source as heat and light can make them turn rancid and affect their colour. For the same reason, buy olive oil in dark green bottles.

Store vinegars in a cool place; they can turn bad in a warm environment.

Store dried herbs, spices and flavourings in a cool, dark cupboard or in dark jars. Buy in small quantities as their flavour will not last indefinitely.

Store flours and sugars in airtight containers.

Refrigerator storage

Fresh food needs to be kept in the cool temperature of the refrigerator to keep it in good condition and discourage the growth of harmful bacteria. Store day-to-day perishable items, such as opened jams and jellies, mayonnaise and bottled sauces, in the refrigerator along with eggs and dairy products, fruit juices, bacon, fresh and cooked meat (on separate shelves), and salads and vegetables (except potatoes, which don't suit being stored in the cold). A refrigerator should be kept at an operating temperature of 4–5°C.

It is worth investing in a refrigerator thermometer to ensure the correct temperature is maintained. To ensure your refrigerator is functioning effectively for safe food storage, follow these guidelines:

To avoid bacterial cross-contamination, store cooked and raw foods on separate shelves, putting cooked foods on the top shelf. Ensure that all items are well wrapped.

Never put hot food into the refrigerator, as this will cause the internal temperature of the refrigerator to rise.

Avoid overfilling the refrigerator, as this restricts the circulation of air and prevents the appliance from working properly.

It can take some time for the refrigerator to return to the correct operating temperature once the door has been opened, so don't leave it open any longer than is necessary.

Clean the refrigerator regularly, using a specially formulated germicidal refrigerator cleaner. Alternatively, use a weak solution of bicarbonate of soda: 1 tbsp to 1 litre (1³/₄ pints) water.

If your refrigerator doesn't have an automatic defrost facility, defrost regularly.

For pre-packed foods, always adhere to the 'use by' date on the packet.

Cookies and Biscuits

Almond Cookies

rice paper to line

2 medium egg whites

200g (7oz) caster sugar

200g (7oz) ground almonds

finely grated zest of 1 orange

$\frac{1}{2}$ tsp ground ginger

40g (1$\frac{1}{2}$oz) stem ginger in syrup, drained and roughly chopped

2 tbsp plain flour, sifted, to dust

12 natural glacé cherries

1 Preheat the oven to 180°C (160°C fan oven) mark 4. Line two baking sheets with rice paper. Put the egg whites in a large bowl and whisk until they form stiff peaks. In another large bowl, stir together the sugar, ground almonds, orange zest, $\frac{1}{4}$ tsp ground ginger and the stem ginger. With a wooden spoon, mix in the egg whites to form a sticky dough.

2 Roll the dough into 12 equal-sized balls. Mix together the flour and the remaining ground ginger in a bowl. Lightly coat each ball in the flour and shake off the excess. Put the balls, spaced well apart, on to the prepared baking sheets. Flatten each one into rounds.

3 Push a glacé cherry in the middle of each cookie and bake for 15–20 minutes until lightly golden.

4 Cool on a wire rack, then trim away the excess rice paper. Store in an airtight container for up to one week.

Try Something Different

Use whole almonds or a sprinkling of orange zest to top each cookie, instead of a glacé cherry.

EASY		NUTRITIONAL INFORMATION		Makes
Preparation Time 15 minutes	**Cooking Time** 15–20 minutes, plus cooling	**Per Cookie** 204 calories, 10g fat (of which 1g saturates), 27g carbohydrate, 0g salt	Vegetarian • Dairy free	**12**

Orange Tuile Biscuits

3 large egg whites
100g (3½oz) icing sugar, sifted
100g (3½oz) plain flour
finely grated zest of 1 orange
75g (3oz) unsalted butter, melted

1 In a large bowl, lightly whisk the egg whites with the sugar. Stir in the flour, orange zest and melted butter, then cover and chill for 30 minutes.

2 Preheat the oven to 200°C (180°C fan oven) mark 6. Line a baking sheet with baking parchment. Put 3 teaspoonfuls of the mixture well apart on the baking sheet and spread out to 9cm (3½in) circles. Bake for 12 minutes or until just brown around the edges.

3 Remove from the oven and, while still warm, shape each biscuit over a rolling pin to curl. Repeat with the remaining mixture. Leave to cool completely on a wire rack.

Makes 24	EASY		NUTRITIONAL INFORMATION	
	Preparation Time 10 minutes, plus 30 minutes chilling	**Cooking Time** 12 minutes, plus cooling	**Per Biscuit** 55 calories, 3g fat (of which 2g saturates), 8g carbohydrate, 0.1g salt	Vegetarian

Try Something Different

Coffee Macaroons: replace 15g (½oz) of the ground almonds with espresso powder and mix together before stirring into the egg mixture.

Macaroons

2 medium egg whites
125g (4oz) caster sugar
125g (4oz) ground almonds
¼ tsp almond extract
22 blanched almonds

1 Preheat the oven to 180°C (160°C fan oven) mark 4 and line two baking sheets with baking parchment. In a large bowl, whisk the egg whites until they form stiff peaks. Gradually fold in the sugar, then gently stir in the almonds and almond extract.

2 Spoon teaspoonfuls of the mixture on to the baking sheets, spacing them slightly apart. Press an almond into each and bake for 12–15 minutes until just golden and firm to the touch.

3 Leave on the baking sheets for 10 minutes, then transfer to a wire rack to cool completely. Store in an airtight container for up to one week.

EASY		NUTRITIONAL INFORMATION		Makes
Preparation Time 10 minutes	**Cooking Time** 12–15 minutes, plus cooling	**Per Macaroon** 73 calories, 3g fat (of which trace saturates), 10g carbohydrate, 0g salt	Vegetarian Gluten free • Dairy free	**22**

Try Something Different

Use dried cherries or dried blueberries instead of the cranberries.
Lemon and Poppy Seed Biscuits: omit the cranberries and add 1 tbsp poppy seeds and the finely grated zest of 1 lemon.

Cranberry Biscuits

125g (4oz) unsalted butter, chilled

50g (2oz) caster sugar

25g (1oz) dried cranberries

125g (4oz) plain flour, sifted, plus extra to dust

75g (3oz) ground rice

1 Whiz the butter and sugar in a food processor, or use an electric hand mixer. Add the cranberries, flour and ground rice, and pulse or beat until the mixture comes together. Turn out on to a lightly floured worksurface and shape into a rectangle about 12.5 x 7.5 x 2cm (5 x 3 x ³⁄₄in). Wrap and chill for 30 minutes.

2 Preheat the oven to 200°C (180°C fan oven) mark 6. Cut the dough into 3mm (¹⁄₈in) slices and put on a non-stick baking sheet. Bake for 8–10 minutes until golden.

3 Leave to cool on the baking sheet. Store in an airtight container for up to one week.

Makes 24	EASY		NUTRITIONAL INFORMATION	
	Preparation Time 15 minutes, plus 30 minutes chilling	**Cooking Time** 8–10 minutes, plus cooling	**Per Biscuit** 79 calories, 4g fat (of which 3g saturates), 10g carbohydrate, 0.1g salt	Vegetarian

Freezing Tip

To serve freshly baked biscuits at another time, open-freeze a tray of unbaked cookies, then pack into bags or containers. Cook from frozen for 18–20 minutes.

Sultana and Pecan Cookies

225g (8oz) unsalted butter, at room temperature, plus extra to grease

175g (6oz) light muscovado sugar

2 medium eggs, lightly beaten

225g (8oz) pecan nut halves

300g (11oz) self-raising flour, sifted

¼ tsp baking powder

125g (4oz) sultanas

2 tbsp maple syrup

1 Preheat the oven to 190°C (170°C fan oven) mark 5 and grease four baking sheets.

2 Cream together the butter and sugar until the mixture is pale and fluffy. Gradually beat in the eggs until thoroughly combined.

3 Put 20 pecan nut halves to one side, then roughly chop the rest and fold into the mixture with the flour, baking powder, sultanas and maple syrup.

4 Roll the mixture into 20 balls and place them, spaced well apart, on the baking sheets. Flatten the cookies with a dampened palette knife and top each with a piece of pecan nut. Bake for 12–15 minutes until pale golden.

5 Leave on the baking sheets for 5 minutes, then transfer to a wire rack to cool completely.

EASY		NUTRITIONAL INFORMATION		Makes
Preparation Time 15 minutes	**Cooking Time** 12–15 minutes, plus cooling	**Per Cookie** 276 calories, 18g fat (of which 7g saturates), 27g carbohydrate, 0.2g salt	Vegetarian	**20**

Try Something Different

Chocolate Nut Cookies: omit the peanut butter and raisins and add 1 tsp vanilla extract. Stir in 175g (6oz) roughly chopped chocolate and 75g (3oz) roughly chopped walnuts.

Coconut and Cherry Cookies: omit the peanut butter and raisins, reduce the sugar to 75g (3oz) and stir in 50g (2oz) desiccated coconut and 125g (4oz) rinsed, roughly chopped glacé cherries.

Oat and Cinnamon Cookies: omit the peanut butter and raisins and add 1 tsp vanilla extract. Stir in 1 tsp ground cinnamon and 75g (3oz) rolled oats.

Peanut and Raisin Cookies

125g (4oz) unsalted butter, softened, plus extra to grease
150g (5oz) caster sugar
1 medium egg
150g (5oz) plain flour, sifted
½ tsp baking powder
½ tsp salt
125g (4oz) crunchy peanut butter
175g (6oz) raisins

1 Preheat the oven to 190°C (170°C fan oven) mark 5 and grease two baking sheets. Beat together all the ingredients except the raisins, until well blended. Stir in the raisins.

2 Spoon large teaspoonfuls of the mixture on to the baking sheets, leaving room for the mixture to spread. Bake for about 15 minutes or until golden brown around the edges.

3 Leave to cool slightly, then transfer to a wire rack to cool completely.

Makes 30	EASY		NUTRITIONAL INFORMATION	
	Preparation Time 10 minutes	**Cooking Time** 15 minutes, plus cooling	**Per Cookie** 111 calories, 6g fat (of which 3g saturates), 14g carbohydrate, 0.2g salt	Vegetarian

Cherry Chip Cookies

75g (3oz) unsalted butter, softened, plus extra to grease

25g (1oz) caster sugar

50g (2oz) light soft brown sugar

a few drops of vanilla extract

1 large egg, lightly beaten

175g (6oz) self-raising flour, sifted

finely grated zest of 1 orange

125g (4oz) white chocolate, roughly broken

125g (4oz) glacé cherries, roughly chopped

icing sugar to dust

1 Preheat the oven to 180°C (160°C fan oven) mark 4 and grease two baking sheets. Beat together the butter, caster sugar, light brown sugar and vanilla extract until well combined, using an electric whisk. Gradually beat in the egg until the mixture is light and fluffy.

2 With a metal spoon, lightly fold in the flour, orange zest, chocolate and glacé cherries. Put tablespoonfuls of the mixture on to the prepared baking sheets and bake for 10–12 minutes. The biscuits should be soft under a crisp crust.

3 Leave the cookies on the baking sheet for 1 minute, then transfer to a wire rack to cool completely. Store in an airtight container for up to three days. Dust with icing sugar just before serving.

EASY			NUTRITIONAL INFORMATION		Makes
Preparation Time 20 minutes	**Cooking Time** 10–12 minutes, plus cooling		**Per Cookie** 179 calories, 8g fat (of which 5g saturates), 27g carbohydrate, 0.1g salt	Vegetarian	**14**

White and Dark Chocolate Cookies

125g (4oz) unsalted butter, softened, plus extra to grease

125g (4oz) golden caster sugar

2 medium eggs, beaten

2 tsp vanilla extract

250g (9oz) self-raising flour, sifted

finely grated zest of 1 orange

100g (3½oz) white chocolate, roughly chopped

100g (3½oz) plain chocolate (at least 70% cocoa solids), roughly chopped

1 Preheat the oven to 180°C (160°C fan oven) mark 4 and grease three baking sheets.

2 Cream together the butter and sugar until the mixture is pale and fluffy. Gradually beat in the eggs and vanilla extract. Sift in the flour, add the orange zest then sprinkle in the white and dark chocolate. Mix the dough together with your hands. Knead lightly, then wrap in clingfilm. Chill the cookie mixture for at least 30 minutes.

3 Divide the mixture into 26 pieces and roll each into a ball. Flatten each ball slightly to make a disc, then put on to the prepared baking sheets, spaced well apart. Bake for about 10–12 minutes until golden.

4 Leave on the baking sheet for 5 minutes, then transfer to a wire rack to cool completely.

Makes 26	EASY		NUTRITIONAL INFORMATION	
	Preparation Time 15 minutes, plus 30 minutes chilling	**Cooking Time** 10–12 minutes, plus cooling	**Per Cookie** 133 calories, 7g fat (of which 4g saturates), 17g carbohydrate, 0.1g salt	Vegetarian

Try Something Different

Vanilla Shortbread Fingers: complete step 1, adding the seeds from 1 vanilla pod to the processor or mixer. Once baked, while warm from the oven mark the shortbread into 24 fingers, sprinkle with caster sugar and cut when cool.

Nutty Fudge Shortbread

225g (8oz) unsalted butter, softened, plus extra to grease

300g (11oz) plain flour, sifted

pinch of salt

125g (4oz) caster sugar

125g (4oz) light muscovado sugar, sifted

2 tbsp golden syrup

170g can condensed milk

300g (11oz) plain chocolate

100g (3½oz) walnut halves

100g (3½oz) hazelnuts, lightly toasted

1 Preheat the oven to 180°C (160°C fan oven) mark 4. Grease a 20.5 x 30.5cm (8 x 12in) Swiss roll tin. Whiz the flour, salt, caster sugar and 150g (5oz) butter in a food processor until it begins to come together. (Alternatively, use a food mixer.) Press the mixture into the prepared tin and smooth over with the back of a spoon. Bake for 20–30 minutes until golden. Leave to cool in the tin.

2 Put the remaining butter, the muscovado sugar, golden syrup and condensed milk in a pan and heat gently but don't boil. Whisk together until combined. Pour over the shortbread, smooth the surface, cool, then chill for 3 hours.

3 Melt the chocolate in a heatproof bowl over a pan of gently simmering water. Stir in the nuts, then pour over the fudge mixture. Smooth the top and leave to set. Cut into 16 pieces to serve.

EASY		NUTRITIONAL INFORMATION		Makes
Preparation Time 40 minutes, plus 3 hours chilling	**Cooking Time** 40 minutes, plus cooling	**Per Serving** 450 calories, 26g fat (of which 12g saturates), 51g carbohydrate, 0.3g salt	Vegetarian	**16**

Cook's Tip

Pipe names on the gift tags and leave the house and tags to set for at least 2 hours. Wrap each gingerbread house in cellophane and tie with ribbon. Attach the gift tags with ribbon.

Gingerbread House

150g (5oz) butter, plus extra to grease
350g (12oz) plain white flour, sifted
1 tsp bicarbonate of soda
2 tbsp ground ginger
200g (7oz) light muscovado sugar
2 tbsp golden syrup
1 medium egg, beaten

For the decoration
200g (7oz) icing sugar, sifted
1 medium egg white
75g (3oz) assorted sweets

Materials
Card to make the three templates:
roof: 10 x 6.5cm (4 x 2½in)
end wall: 10 x 6cm (4 x 2¼in)
side wall: 6 x 8cm (2¼ x 3¼in)
four 15cm (6in) cake boards covered in paper
ribbon and cellophane

1 Grease two baking sheets. Cut the card into templates for the roof and walls. Put the flour, bicarbonate of soda and ginger into a bowl. Rub in the butter until the mixture resembles breadcrumbs. Stir in the sugar. Warm the golden syrup in a pan, pour on to the flour with the beaten egg and stir. Bring together into a soft dough and knead until smooth. Divide into four pieces, wrap in clingfilm and chill for 15 minutes.

2 Roll out one piece of dough to 3mm (⅛in) thick. Cut out two of each template. Put on to the baking sheets. Repeat with the remaining dough. Stamp out four hearts from the trimmings and skewer a hole in the top of each. Put on to the baking sheets. Chill for 15 minutes. Preheat the oven to 190°C (170°C fan oven) mark 5. Bake for 8–10 minutes until golden. While still warm, push a skewer through the holes. Leave on the baking sheets for 5 minutes, then transfer to a wire rack to cool completely.

3 To decorate, beat the icing sugar into the egg white until the mixture stands in peaks. Spoon into a piping bag and pipe windows and doors on the walls and squiggly lines on the roof. Leave to dry for 2 hours. Pipe icing along the edge of the side walls and stick to the end walls. Leave to dry for 1 hour, then place on a board and fill with sweets. Pipe icing along the top of each house and the roof pieces and press gently in position; hold for 1–2 minutes until secure.

Makes	A LITTLE EFFORT		NUTRITIONAL INFORMATION	
4 houses	**Preparation Time** 4 hours, plus 30 minutes chilling and 5 hours drying	**Cooking Time** 10 minutes	**Per House** 1000 calories, 34g fat (of which 20g saturates), 172g carbohydrate, 0.7g salt	Vegetarian

Hazelnut and Chocolate Biscotti

125g (4oz) plain flour, sifted, plus extra to dust
75g (3oz) golden caster sugar
¼ tsp baking powder
a pinch of cinnamon
a pinch of salt
1 large egg, beaten
1 tbsp milk
¼ tsp vanilla extract
25g (1oz) hazelnuts
25g (1oz) plain chocolate chips

1 Preheat the oven to 200°C (180°C fan oven) mark 6. Put the flour into a large bowl. Stir in the sugar, baking powder, cinnamon and salt. Make a well in the centre and stir in the beaten egg, milk, vanilla extract, hazelnuts and chocolate chips with a fork to form a sticky dough.

2 On a lightly floured surface, gently knead the mixture into a ball. Roll into a 28cm (11in) log shape. Put on a baking sheet and flatten slightly. Bake for 20–25 minutes or until pale golden.

3 Turn down the oven temperature to 150°C (130°C fan oven) mark 2. Put the biscotti log on to a chopping board and slice diagonally with a bread knife at 1cm (½in) intervals. Arrange the slices on the baking sheet and put back in the oven for 15 minutes or until golden and dry. Transfer to a wire rack to cool completely. Store in an airtight container for up to one month.

Makes 20	EASY		NUTRITIONAL INFORMATION	
	Preparation Time 10 minutes	**Cooking Time** 35–40 minutes, plus cooling	**Per Biscuit** 50 calories, 1g fat (of which trace saturates), 9g carbohydrate, 0g salt	Vegetarian

Try Something Different

Cranberry, Hazelnut and Orange Biscotti: increase the flour to 375g (13oz), omit the cocoa powder and add the grated zest of 1 orange. Replace the chocolate chips with dried cranberries and the pistachios with chopped blanched hazelnuts.

Chocolate and Pistachio Biscotti

300g (11oz) plain flour, sifted

75g (3oz) cocoa powder, sifted

1 tsp baking powder

150g (5oz) plain chocolate chips

150g (5oz) shelled pistachio nuts

a pinch of salt

75g (3oz) unsalted butter, softened

225g (8oz) granulated sugar

2 large eggs, beaten

1 tbsp icing sugar

1 Preheat the oven to 180°C (160°C fan oven) mark 4 and line a large baking sheet with baking parchment. Mix together the flour, cocoa powder, baking powder, chocolate chips, pistachio nuts and salt.

2 Using an electric whisk, beat together the butter and granulated sugar until light and fluffy. Gradually whisk in the beaten eggs.

3 Stir the dry ingredients into the mixture until it forms a stiff dough. With floured hands, shape the dough into two slightly flattened logs, each about 30.5 x 5cm (12 x 2in). Sprinkle with icing sugar. Put the logs on to the prepared baking sheet and bake for 40–45 minutes until they are slightly firm to the touch.

4 Leave the logs on the baking sheet for 10 minutes, then cut diagonally into 2cm (³/₄in) thick slices. Arrange them, cut side down, on the baking sheet and bake again for 15 minutes or until crisp. Cool on a wire rack.

EASY		NUTRITIONAL INFORMATION		Makes
Preparation Time 15 minutes	**Cooking Time** about 1 hour, plus cooling	**Per Biscuit** 152 calories, 7g fat (of which 3g saturates), 20g carbohydrate, 0.2g salt	Vegetarian	**30**

Spiced Star Biscuits

2 tbsp runny honey
25g (1oz) unsalted butter
50g (2oz) light muscovado sugar
finely grated zest of ½ lemon
finely grated zest of ½ orange
225g (8oz) self-raising flour, plus extra to roll out
1 tsp ground cinnamon
1 tsp ground ginger
½ tsp freshly grated nutmeg
pinch of ground cloves
a pinch of salt
1 tbsp finely chopped candied peel
50g (2oz) ground almonds
1 large egg, beaten
1½ tbsp milk

For the decoration
150g (5oz) icing sugar
silver sugar balls

1 Put the honey, butter, muscovado sugar and citrus zests into a small pan and stir over a low heat until the butter has melted and the ingredients are well combined.

2 Sift the flour, spices and salt together into a bowl, then add the chopped candied peel and ground almonds. Add the melted mixture, beaten egg and milk and mix until the dough comes together. Knead the dough briefly until smooth, then wrap in clingfilm and chill for at least 4 hours, or overnight.

3 Preheat the oven to 180°C (160°C fan oven) mark 4. Roll out the dough on a lightly floured surface to 5mm (¼in) thick. Using a 5cm (2in) cutter, stamp out stars and put on to baking sheets. Bake for 15–20 minutes or until just beginning to brown at the edges.

4 Transfer the biscuits to a wire rack to cool.

5 To decorate, mix the icing sugar with 1½ tbsp warm water to make a smooth icing. Coat some of the biscuits with icing and finish with a piped edging if you like, then decorate with silver balls. Pipe dots of icing on the plain biscuits and attach silver balls. Allow the icing to set, then store the biscuits in an airtight container for up to one week.

EASY		NUTRITIONAL INFORMATION		Makes
Preparation Time 15 minutes, plus 4 hours chilling	**Cooking Time** 15–20 minutes, plus cooling	**Per Biscuit** 51 calories, 2g fat (of which 1g saturates), 8g carbohydrate, 0g salt	Vegetarian	**35**

2

Brownies and Bars

Cook's Tip

The secret to really moist, squidgy brownies is all in the timing. A few minutes too long in the oven will produce a dry texture so be careful not to overbake them.

The Ultimate Chocolate Brownie

200g (7oz) butter, plus extra to grease

400g (14oz) plain chocolate

225g (8oz) light muscovado sugar

1 tsp vanilla extract

150g (5oz) pecan nuts, roughly chopped

25g (1oz) cocoa powder, sifted, plus extra to dust (optional)

75g (3oz) self-raising flour, sifted

3 large eggs, beaten

1 Preheat the oven to 170°C (150°C fan oven) mark 3. Grease a 20.5cm (8in) square shallow cake tin and line the base with non-stick baking parchment. Put the butter and chocolate in a heatproof bowl over a pan of gently simmering water and stir until melted. Remove from the heat and stir in the sugar, vanilla extract, pecan nuts, cocoa, flour and eggs.

2 Turn the mixture into the prepared tin and level the surface with the back of a spoon. Bake for about 1 hour 15 minutes or until set on the surface but still soft underneath.

3 Leave to cool in the tin for 2 hours. Turn out, dust with sifted cocoa powder, if using, and cut into squares. Eat cold or serve warm with ice cream.

Makes 16	EASY		NUTRITIONAL INFORMATION	
	Preparation Time 15 minutes	**Cooking Time** 1 hour 20 minutes, plus 2 hours cooling	**Per Brownie** 257 calories, 11g fat (of which 6g saturates), 38g carbohydrate, 0.2g salt	Vegetarian

Chocolate Fudge Brownies

butter to grease

125g (4oz) milk chocolate

9 ready-to-eat prunes

200g (7oz) light muscovado sugar

3 large egg whites

1 tsp vanilla extract

75g (3oz) plain flour, sifted

50g (2oz) white chocolate, chopped

icing sugar to dust

1 Preheat the oven to 180°C (160°C fan oven) mark 4. Grease and baseline a 15cm (6in) square shallow cake tin. Melt the milk chocolate in a heatproof bowl over a pan of gently simmering water. Remove from the heat and leave to cool slightly.

2 Put the prunes in a food processor or blender with 100ml (3½fl oz) water and whiz for 2–3 minutes to make a purée. Add the muscovado sugar and whiz briefly to mix.

3 In a clean, grease-free bowl, whisk the egg whites until they form soft peaks.

4 Add the vanilla extract, prune mixture, flour, white chocolate and egg whites to the bowl of melted chocolate. Fold everything together gently. Pour the mixture into the prepared tin and bake for 1 hour or until firm to the touch.

5 Leave to cool in the tin. Turn out, dust with icing sugar and cut into 12 squares.

EASY		NUTRITIONAL INFORMATION		Makes
Preparation Time 20 minutes	**Cooking Time** 1 hour, plus cooling	**Per Brownie** 174 calories, 5g fat (of which 3g saturates), 33g carbohydrate, 0.1g salt	Vegetarian	**12**

Double-chocolate Brownies

250g (9oz) butter, plus extra to grease

250g (9oz) plain chocolate (at least 50% cocoa solids), broken into pieces

100g (3½oz) white chocolate, broken into pieces

4 medium eggs

175g (6oz) light muscovado sugar

1 tsp vanilla extract

75g (3oz) plain flour, sifted

¼ tsp baking powder

1 tbsp cocoa powder, sifted, plus extra to dust

100g (3½oz) pecan nuts, chopped

a pinch of salt

a little icing sugar to dust

1 Preheat the oven to 200°C (180°C fan oven) mark 6. Grease and baseline a 20.5cm (8in) square shallow tin. Melt the butter and plain chocolate in a heatproof bowl over a pan of gently simmering water. Remove the bowl from the pan and put to one side.

2 In a separate bowl, melt the white chocolate over a pan of gently simmering water. Put to one side.

3 Put the eggs into a separate large bowl. Add the muscovado sugar and vanilla extract, and whisk together until the mixture is pale and thick.

4 Add the flour, baking powder, cocoa powder, pecan nuts and a pinch of salt to the bowl, then carefully pour in the dark chocolate mixture. Gently fold the ingredients together using a large metal spoon to make a smooth batter. If you fold too roughly, the chocolate will seize up.

5 Pour the brownie mixture into the tin. Spoon dollops of the white chocolate over the brownie mix, then swirl a skewer through it several times to create a marbled effect. Bake for 20–25 minutes. The brownies should still be fudgy inside and the top should be cracked and crispy.

6 Leave to cool in the tin. Transfer the brownies to a board and cut into 16 pieces. To serve, dust with a little icing sugar and cocoa powder.

Try Something Different

Try making these brownies without butter – believe it or not, this recipe will still work. But you'll need to eat them within an hour of taking them out of the oven – fat is what makes cakes moist and helps them keep.

EASY		NUTRITIONAL INFORMATION		Makes
Preparation Time 15 minutes	**Cooking Time** 20–25 minutes, plus cooling	**Per Brownie** 352 calories, 25g fat (of which 13g saturates), 29g carbohydrate, 0.3g salt	Vegetarian	**16**

Freezing Tip

Complete the recipe up to the end of step 2. Remove from the tin, wrap and freeze.
To use Thaw at cool room temperature for about 5 hours. Complete the recipe.

Cherry Chocolate Fudge Brownies

150g (5oz) unsalted butter, plus extra to grease
200g (7oz) plain chocolate (70% cocoa solids)
175g (6oz) caster sugar
2 tsp vanilla extract
5 medium eggs
175g (6oz) plain flour
³/₄ tsp baking powder
250g (9oz) glacé cherries, halved

For the icing
150g (5oz) plain chocolate (70% cocoa solids)
2 tbsp Kirsch
4 tbsp double cream

1 Preheat the oven to 180°C (160°C fan oven) mark 4. Grease and baseline an 18cm (7in) square shallow cake tin. Put the butter and chocolate in a heatproof bowl over a pan of gently simmering water. Leave the chocolate to melt without stirring. Remove the bowl from the pan and stir until smooth. Leave to cool.

2 In a bowl, whisk the sugar, vanilla extract and eggs until pale and thick. Stir the chocolate into the egg mixture. Sift the flour and baking powder together and lightly fold into the mixture with the cherries. Pour the mixture into the prepared tin. Bake for 40 minutes or until just set. Cool slightly in the tin before icing.

3 To make the icing, put the chocolate and Kirsch in a heatproof bowl over a pan of gently simmering water. Once melted, add the cream and 4 tbsp water, and stir well. Pour over the brownie and leave to set. Cut into 12 squares.

Makes 12	EASY		NUTRITIONAL INFORMATION	
	Preparation Time 20 minutes	**Cooking Time** 50 minutes, plus cooling and 1 hour setting	**Per Brownie** 462 calories, 24g fat (of which 14g saturates), 59g carbohydrate, 0.3g salt	Vegetarian

White Chocolate and Nut Brownies

75g (3oz) unsalted butter, plus extra to grease

500g (1lb 2oz) white chocolate, roughly chopped

3 large eggs

175g (6oz) golden caster sugar

175g (6oz) self-raising flour

a pinch of salt

175g (6oz) macadamia nuts, roughly chopped

1 tsp vanilla extract

1 Preheat the oven to 190°C (170°C fan oven) mark 5. Grease and line a 25.5 x 20.5cm (10 x 8in) baking tin.

2 Melt 125g (4oz) white chocolate with the butter in a heatproof bowl over a pan of gently simmering water, stirring occasionally. Remove the bowl from the pan and leave to cool slightly.

3 Whisk the eggs and sugar together in a large bowl until smooth, then gradually beat in the melted chocolate mixture; the consistency will become quite firm. Sift the flour and salt over the mixture, then fold in with the nuts, the remaining chopped chocolate and the vanilla extract.

4 Turn the mixture into the prepared tin and level the surface. Bake for 30–35 minutes until risen and golden and the centre is just firm to the touch – the mixture will still be soft under the crust; it firms up on cooling. Leave to cool in the tin. Turn out and cut into 12 squares. Store in an airtight container for up to one week.

EASY		NUTRITIONAL INFORMATION		Makes
Preparation Time 20 minutes	**Cooking Time** 30–35 minutes, plus cooling	**Per Brownie** 502 calories, 31g fat (of which 13g saturates), 52g carbohydrate, 0.4g salt	Vegetarian	**12**

Low-fat Brownies

50ml (2fl oz) sunflower oil, plus extra to grease

250g (9oz) plain chocolate (at least 50% cocoa solids)

4 medium eggs

150g (5oz) light muscovado sugar

1 tsp vanilla extract

75g (3oz) plain flour

¼ tsp baking powder

1 tbsp cocoa powder

1 Preheat the oven to 200°C (180°C fan oven) mark 6. Grease and line a 20.5cm (8in) square shallow tin.

2 Melt the chocolate in a heatproof bowl over a pan of gently simmering water. Remove the bowl from the pan and put to one side to cool slightly.

3 Put the eggs into a large bowl, add the sunflower oil, sugar and vanilla extract, and whisk together until pale and thick. Sift the flour, baking powder and cocoa powder into the bowl, then carefully pour in the chocolate. Using a large metal spoon, gently fold all the ingredients together – if you fold too roughly, the chocolate will seize up and become unusable.

4 Carefully pour the brownie mixture into the prepared tin and bake for 20 minutes – when cooked, the brownies should still be fudgy in the centre and the top should be cracked and crispy. Cut into 16 squares immediately, then leave to cool in the tin. To store, wrap in clingfilm and store in an airtight container for up to three days.

Makes 16	EASY		NUTRITIONAL INFORMATION	
	Preparation Time 10 minutes	**Cooking Time** 20 minutes, plus cooling	**Per Brownie** 172 calories, 8g fat (of which 3g saturates), 24g carbohydrate, 0.1g salt	Vegetarian • Dairy free

Try Something Different

Tropical Fruit and Coconut Flapjacks: replace the hazelnuts and chocolate with chopped, dried mixed tropical fruit. Replace 50g (2oz) of the oats with desiccated coconut.

Apricot and Mixed Seed Flapjacks: replace the hazelnuts with 50g (2oz) mixed seeds (such as pumpkin, sunflower, linseed and sesame). Reduce the oats to 125g (4oz) and replace the chocolate with 100g (3½oz) chopped dried apricots.

Hazelnut and Chocolate Flapjacks

125g (4oz) unsalted butter, plus extra to grease
125g (4oz) light muscovado sugar
1 tbsp golden syrup
50g (2oz) hazelnuts, roughly chopped
175g (6oz) jumbo or porridge oats
50g (2oz) plain chocolate, roughly chopped

1 Preheat the oven to 180°C (160°C fan oven) mark 4. Lightly grease a 28 x 18cm (11 x 7in) shallow baking tin.

2 Melt together the butter, sugar and golden syrup. Stir in the hazelnuts and oats. Leave the mixture to cool slightly, then stir in the chocolate.

3 Spoon the mixture into the prepared tin and bake for about 30 minutes or until golden and firm.

4 Leave to cool in the tin for a few minutes, then cut into 12 pieces. Turn out on to a wire rack and leave to cool completely. Store in an airtight container for up to one week.

EASY		NUTRITIONAL INFORMATION		Makes
Preparation Time 10 minutes	**Cooking Time** 30 minutes, plus cooling	**Per Flapjack** 229 calories, 14g fat (of which 6g saturates), 26g carbohydrate, 0.2g salt	Vegetarian	**12**

Try Something Different

Date and Banana Bars: omit the chocolate chips, pecan nuts and chocolate spread. Instead, put 175g (6oz) chopped dates in a pan with the zest and juice of 1 lemon and 2 tbsp water. Simmer gently for about 4 minutes or until tender. Cool slightly. Blend 1 roughly chopped banana with the mixture at step 3; fold in the date mixture.

Chocolate Pecan Bars

125g (4oz) plain flour, sifted
25g (1oz) icing sugar
200g (7oz) unsalted butter, plus extra to grease
1 large egg yolk and 2 large eggs
125g (4oz) self-raising flour
1 tsp baking powder
125g (4oz) caster sugar
3–4 drops vanilla extract
150g (5oz) milk chocolate chips
75g (3oz) pecan nuts, chopped
6 tbsp chocolate and hazelnut spread

1 Preheat the oven to 200°C (180°C fan oven) mark 6. Grease and baseline a 25.5 x 15cm (10 x 6in) shallow baking tin.

2 Put the plain flour and icing sugar in a food processor with 75g (3oz) roughly chopped butter and whiz until crumb-like in texture. (Alternatively, rub the butter into the dry ingredients in a large bowl by hand or using a pastry cutter.) Add the egg yolk and whiz for 10–15 seconds, or add to the bowl with the dry ingredients and stir until the mixture begins to come together. Turn into the tin and press into a thin layer. Bake for 15 minutes or until golden.

3 Meanwhile, put the self-raising flour, baking powder, caster sugar, vanilla extract and the remaining eggs in the food processor with the remaining softened butter and blend for 15 seconds or until smooth, or put the ingredients into a bowl and mix well with a wooden spoon. Remove the blade and fold in the chocolate chips and pecan nuts. Set aside.

4 Spread the chocolate and hazelnut spread over the cooked base and top with the cake mixture. Reduce the oven temperature to 180°C (160°C fan oven) mark 4 and bake for 45–50 minutes until golden – cover loosely with foil if necessary. Leave to cool in the tin for about 10 minutes, then turn out on to a wire rack to cool completely. Cut into 25 pieces and store in an airtight container for up to two days.

Makes 25	EASY		NUTRITIONAL INFORMATION	
	Preparation Time 15 minutes	**Cooking Time** 1¼ hours, plus cooling	**Per Bar** 189 calories, 13g fat (of which 6g saturates), 18g carbohydrate, 0.2g salt	Vegetarian

Cook's Tip

Don't overcook the flapjacks or they will be hard and dry. When they are cooked, they should still be sticky and slightly soft when you press them in the middle.

Sticky Ginger Flapjacks

350g (12oz) unsalted butter, plus extra to grease

275g (10oz) caster sugar

225g (8oz) golden syrup

450g (1lb) rolled oats

1 tbsp ground ginger

1 Preheat the oven to 180°C (160°C fan oven) mark 4. Grease and baseline a 28 x 18cm (11 x 7in) shallow cake tin with non-stick baking parchment. Put the butter, sugar and golden syrup in a large pan and heat them together gently until melted. Mix in the rolled oats and ground ginger until they are thoroughly combined.

2 Pour the mixture into the tin, level the surface and bake for 30–35 minutes until golden brown around the edges.

3 Leave to cool in the tin for 15 minutes. While still warm, score into 24 pieces with a sharp knife. Leave in the tin to cool completely, then turn out and cut out the pieces.

Makes 24	EASY		NUTRITIONAL INFORMATION	
	Preparation Time 10 minutes	**Cooking Time** 40 minutes, plus cooling	**Per Flapjack** 259 calories, 14g fat (of which 8g saturates), 33g carbohydrate, 0.3g salt	Vegetarian

Apple Shorties

75g (3oz) unsalted butter, softened, plus extra to grease

40g (1½oz) caster sugar

75g (3oz) plain flour, sifted

40g (1½oz) fine semolina

1 cooking apple, about 175g (6oz), peeled and grated

125g (4oz) sultanas

½ tsp mixed spice

2 tbsp light muscovado sugar

1 tsp lemon juice

1 Preheat the oven to 190°C (170°C fan oven) mark 5, and grease an 18cm (7in) square shallow cake tin.

2 Beat together the butter, caster sugar, flour and semolina until the mixture is blended. Press the mixture into the prepared tin and level the surface. Bake for 15 minutes.

3 Meanwhile, mix the apple with the remaining ingredients. Spoon evenly over the shortbread and put back in the oven for a further 15 minutes. Leave to cool in the tin for a few minutes, then cut into 16 squares. Leave to cool completely, then remove from the tin.

EASY		NUTRITIONAL INFORMATION		Makes
Preparation Time 20 minutes	**Cooking Time** 30 minutes, plus cooling	**Per Square** 100 calories, 4g fat (of which 3g saturates), 17g carbohydrate, 0.1g salt	Vegetarian	**16**

Chilled Chocolate Biscuit Cake

125g (4oz) unsalted butter, chopped, plus extra to grease
150g (5oz) plain chocolate, broken into pieces
250g (9oz) panforte, chopped
100g (3½ oz) Rich Tea biscuits, chopped
2–3 tbsp Amaretto, rum or brandy
ice cream to serve (optional)

1 Grease an 18cm (7in) square cake tin and baseline with baking parchment. Put the butter and chocolate in a heatproof bowl over a pan of gently simmering water. Stir until melted, then set aside.

2 In a large bowl, mix the panforte, biscuits and liqueur, rum or brandy. Add the melted chocolate mixture and stir to coat.

3 Pour the mixture into the cake tin and chill for at least 2 hours. Cut into wedges and serve with ice cream if you like.

Cook's Tip

Panforte is a flat Italian cake, a mixture of dried fruit and nuts, bound with honey and baked on rice paper. It is a Christmas speciality, so look for it in Italian delicatessens and larger supermarkets from November to January.

EASY		NUTRITIONAL INFORMATION		Makes
Preparation Time 15 minutes, plus 2 hours chilling	**Cooking Time** 5 minutes	**Per Wedge** 157 calories, 9g fat (of which 5g saturates), 17g carbohydrate, 0.3g salt	Vegetarian	**21**

500g (1lb 2oz) ready-to-eat dried figs, hard stalks removed

50g (2oz) candied orange peel, finely chopped

75g (3oz) hazelnuts, toasted

50g (2oz) shelled pistachio nuts

50g (2oz) plain chocolate, broken into pieces

50g (2oz) ready-to-eat pitted dates

$\frac{1}{4}$ tsp ground cinnamon

a pinch of freshly grated nutmeg

4 tbsp brandy, plus extra to drizzle

rice paper

Figgy Fruit Slice

1 Put the figs and candied orange peel in a food processor and whiz for 1 minute to mince the fruit finely. Tip into a large bowl.

2 Put the hazelnuts, pistachio nuts, chocolate and dates in the food processor with the spices and 4 tbsp brandy and pulse to chop roughly. Add to the fig mixture and mix, using your hands.

3 Put a sheet of rice paper on a baking sheet. Spoon the fig mixture evenly on top, then press down with the back of a wet spoon to form an even layer about 2cm ($\frac{3}{4}$in) thick. Put another sheet of rice paper on top and press down well. Chill for 1 hour.

4 Cut the slice into four rectangles to serve. If not serving straightaway, wrap in baking parchment and tie up with string. Store in the refrigerator for up to four weeks, unwrapping and drizzling with 1 tsp brandy every week.

Serves 4	EASY		NUTRITIONAL INFORMATION	
	Preparation Time 30 minutes, plus chilling	**Cooking Time** 10 minutes	**Per Serving** 577 calories, 20g fat (of which 4g saturates), 86g carbohydrate, 0.4g salt	Vegetarian Gluten free • Dairy free

Try Something Different

Cherry and Coconut Crumble Bars: rinse and dry 225g (8oz) glacé cherries and quarter them; fold the cherries into the crumble topping at the end of step 2. Make the sponge base as in step 3, adding 50g (2oz) desiccated coconut to the ingredients.

Vanilla Crumble Bars

250g (9oz) unsalted butter, softened, plus extra to grease

250g (9oz) caster sugar

125g (4oz) plain flour, sifted

175g (6oz) self-raising flour

grated zest of 1 lemon

3 large eggs

1½ tsp vanilla extract

1 Preheat the oven to 180°C (160°C fan oven) mark 4. Grease and line a 25.5 x 18cm (10 x 7in) shallow baking tin.

2 To make the crumble topping, put 75g (3oz) of the butter and 75g (3oz) of the sugar in a food processor and blend until smooth. Add the plain flour and blend for 8–10 seconds until the mixture forms very rough breadcrumbs, then put to one side.

3 Put the remaining butter and sugar, the self-raising flour, lemon zest, eggs and vanilla extract in the food processor and whiz for about 15 seconds or until smooth. Pour the mixture into the prepared tin, sprinkle the crumble topping over the surface and press down to cover.

4 Bake for 50–60 minutes, covering loosely with foil for the last 10 minutes if the mixture is browning too much. Leave in the tin for 5 minutes, then turn out on to a wire rack. Cut into 25 bars and store in an airtight container for up to three days.

EASY		NUTRITIONAL INFORMATION		Makes
Preparation Time 15 minutes	**Cooking Time** 50–60 minutes, plus cooling	**Per Bar** 295 calories, 10g fat (of which 5g saturates), 50g carbohydrate, 0.6g salt	Vegetarian	**25**

3

Small Cakes and Muffins

125g (4oz) unsalted butter, at room temperature

125g (4oz) golden caster sugar

1 vanilla pod

2 medium eggs

125g (4oz) self-raising flour, sifted

1 tbsp vanilla extract

200g (7oz) white chocolate, in small pieces

Vanilla and White Chocolate Cup Cakes

For the frosted flowers

1 medium egg white

6 edible violets

caster sugar to dust

1 Preheat the oven to 190°C (170°C fan oven) mark 5. Line a bun tin with 12 paper muffin cases.

2 Put the butter and sugar in a bowl. Split the vanilla pod lengthways, scrape out the seeds and add to the bowl. Add the eggs, flour and vanilla extract, and beat thoroughly, using an electric whisk, until smooth and creamy. Spoon the mixture into the muffin cases and bake for 15–20 minutes until pale golden, risen and springy to the touch. Leave in the tin for 2–3 minutes, then transfer to a wire rack to cool.

3 To make the frosted flowers, whisk the egg white in a clean bowl for 30 seconds until frothy. Brush over the violet petals and put on a wire rack. Lightly dust with caster sugar and leave to dry.

4 Melt the chocolate in a heatproof bowl set over a pan of gently simmering water. Stir until smooth and leave to cool slightly. Spoon the chocolate on to the cakes, top with a frosted flower and leave to set.

Makes 12	EASY		NUTRITIONAL INFORMATION	
	Preparation Time 25 minutes	**Cooking Time** 15–20 minutes, plus cooling	**Per Cake** 270 calories, 15g fat (of which 9g saturates), 32g carbohydrate, 0.2g salt	Vegetarian

Chocolate Cup Cakes

125g (4oz) unsalted butter, softened
125g (4oz) light muscovado sugar
2 medium eggs, beaten
15g (½oz) cocoa powder
100g (3½oz) self-raising flour
100g (3½oz) plain chocolate (at least 70% cocoa solids),
roughly chopped

For the topping
150ml (¼ pint) double cream
100g (3½oz) plain chocolate (at least 70% cocoa solids),
broken up

1 Preheat the oven to 190°C (170°C fan oven) mark 5. Line bun tins or muffin pans with 18 paper muffin cases.

2 Beat together the butter and sugar until light and fluffy. Gradually beat in the eggs. Sift the cocoa powder with the flour and fold into the creamed mixture with the chopped chocolate.

3 Divide the mixture among the paper cases and lightly flatten the surface with the back of a spoon. Bake for 20 minutes. Cool in the cases.

4 For the topping, put the cream and broken-up chocolate into a heavy-based pan over a low heat and heat until melted, then allow to cool and thicken slightly. Pour over the cooled cakes and leave to set for 30 minutes.

EASY		NUTRITIONAL INFORMATION		Makes
Preparation Time 15 minutes	**Cooking Time** 20 minutes, plus cooling and setting	**Per Cake** 203 calories, 14g fat (of which 8g saturates), 19g carbohydrate, 0.2g salt	Vegetarian	**18**

Dainty Cup Cakes

175g (6oz) unsalted butter, softened

175g (6oz) golden caster sugar

3 medium eggs

175g (6oz) self-raising flour, sifted

finely grated zest and juice of 1 lemon

For the frosted flowers

1 medium egg white

6 edible flowers, such as violas

caster sugar to dust

For the icing

225g (8oz) icing sugar, sifted

1 drop violet food colouring

2–3 tbsp lemon juice, strained

1 Preheat the oven to 190°C (170°C fan oven) mark 5. Line a bun tin or muffin pan with 12 paper muffin cases.

2 Put the butter and caster sugar in a bowl and cream together until pale, light and fluffy. Add the eggs, one at a time, and beat together, folding 1 tbsp flour into the mixture if it looks as if it is going to curdle. Fold in the flour, lemon zest and juice, and mix everything well.

3 Spoon the mixture into the cases and bake for 15–20 minutes until pale golden, risen and springy to the touch. Cool on a wire rack.

4 To make the frosted flowers, whisk the egg white in a clean bowl for 30 seconds until frothy. Brush over the flower petals and put on a wire rack resting on a piece of greaseproof paper. Dust heavily with caster sugar, then leave the flowers to dry.

5 To make the icing, put the icing sugar into a bowl with the violet food colouring. Mix in the lemon juice to make a smooth dropping consistency. Spoon the icing on to the cakes. Decorate with the frosted flowers and leave until the icing is set.

Try Something Different

Ginger and Orange Cup Cakes: replace the lemon zest and juice with orange and add two pieces of preserved stem ginger, drained and chopped. Omit the frosted flowers and make the icing with orange juice instead of lemon. Decorate with finely chopped stem ginger.

EASY		NUTRITIONAL INFORMATION		Makes
Preparation Time 15 minutes	**Cooking Time** 15–20 minutes, plus cooling	**Per Cake** 306 calories, 14g fat (of which 8g saturates), 46g carbohydrate, 0.4g salt	Vegetarian	**12**

Sour Cherry Cakes

175g (6oz) unsalted butter, softened
175g (6oz) golden caster sugar
3 medium eggs
175g (6oz) self-raising flour, sifted
75g (3oz) dried cherries
2 tbsp milk
225g (8oz) golden icing sugar, sifted
3 tbsp lemon juice, strained

1 Preheat the oven to 190°C (170°C fan oven) mark 5. Line a bun tin or muffin pan with 12 paper muffin cases.

2 Put the butter and caster sugar in a bowl and cream together until pale, light and fluffy. Beat in the eggs, one at a time, folding in 1 tbsp flour if the mixture looks like it is starting to curdle.

3 Put 12 dried cherries to one side. Fold the remaining flour, cherries and the milk into the creamed mixture until evenly combined. Spoon the mixture into the paper cases and bake for 15–20 minutes until pale golden and risen. Remove from the tin and cool on a wire rack.

4 Put the icing sugar in a bowl and mix with the lemon juice to make a smooth dropping consistency. Spoon on to the cakes and decorate each with a cherry.

Makes 12	EASY		NUTRITIONAL INFORMATION	
	Preparation Time 30 minutes	Cooking Time 15–20 minutes, plus cooling	Per Cake 323 calories, 14g fat (of which 8g saturates), 50g carbohydrate, 0.4g salt	Vegetarian

Try Something Different

....

Lemon Madeleines: omit the vanilla extract and apples. Stir 2 tbsp clear honey into the warm melted butter, then leave to cool. Add the grated zest of 1 lemon together with the flour.

Apple Madeleines

150g (5oz) unsalted butter, melted and cooled, plus extra to grease

3 large eggs

150g (5oz) caster sugar

1 tsp vanilla extract

150g (5oz) plain flour, sifted

½ tsp baking powder

2 apples such as Cox's, peeled, cored and finely chopped

icing sugar to dust

1 Preheat the oven to 200°C (180°C fan oven) mark 6. Grease the madeleine tins.

2 Using an electric whisk, beat the eggs and caster sugar together until pale and thick (this should take about 8 minutes), then add the vanilla extract. Quickly but gently, fold in the flour, baking powder and apples followed by the melted butter, making sure the butter doesn't settle at the bottom of the bowl.

3 Spoon the mixture into the madeleine tins. Bake for 8–10 minutes until golden, then remove from the tins and cool on a wire rack. Store in an airtight container for up to two days. Dust with icing sugar before serving.

EASY		NUTRITIONAL INFORMATION		Makes
Preparation Time 15 minutes	**Cooking Time** 8–10 minutes, plus cooling	**Per Madeleine** 106 calories, 6g fat (of which 4g saturates), 13g carbohydrate, 0.1g salt	Vegetarian	**24**

225g (8oz) plain flour

1 tsp baking powder

a pinch of salt

75g (3oz) caster sugar

50g (2oz) ground almonds

350g (12oz) glacé cherries, roughly chopped

300ml (½ pint) milk

3 tbsp lemon juice

50ml (2fl oz) sunflower oil or melted butter

1 large egg

1 tsp almond extract

roughly crushed sugar cubes to decorate

Cherry and Almond Muffins

1 Preheat the oven to 190°C (170°C fan oven) mark 5. Line a bun tin with 12 paper muffin cases.

2 Sift together the flour, baking powder and salt. Add the caster sugar and ground almonds. Stir in the chopped cherries.

3 Whisk together the milk, lemon juice, oil or butter, the egg and almond extract. Pour into the dry ingredients and stir tuntil all the ingredients are just combined – the mixture should be lumpy. Do not overmix or the muffins will be tough.

4 Spoon the mixture into the muffin cases. Sprinkle with the crushed sugar cubes and bake for about 25 minutes until well risen and golden.

5 Leave the muffins to cool in the tin for 5 minutes, then transfer to a wire rack to cool completely. These muffins are best eaten on the day they are made.

Makes 12	EASY		NUTRITIONAL INFORMATION	
	Preparation Time 10 minutes	**Cooking Time** 25 minutes, plus cooling	**Per Muffin** 230 calories, 6g fat (of which 1g saturates), 42g carbohydrate, 0.1g salt	Vegetarian

Try Something Different

Apple and Cinnamon Muffins: fold 5 tbsp ready-made chunky apple sauce and 1 tsp ground cinnamon into the mixture with the flour.

Maple Syrup and Pecan Muffins: lightly toast 50g (2oz) pecan nuts and roughly chop. Fold half the nuts and 3 tbsp maple syrup into the mixture. Mix the remaining nuts with the crushed sugar and sprinkle over the muffins before baking. Drizzle with maple syrup to serve.

Brown Sugar Muffins

12 brown sugar cubes
150g (5oz) plain flour
1½ tsp baking powder
¼ tsp salt
1 medium egg, beaten
40g (1½oz) golden caster sugar
50g (2oz) unsalted butter, melted
½ tsp vanilla extract
100ml (3½fl oz) milk

1 Preheat the oven to 200°C (180°C fan oven) mark 6. Line a bun tin or muffin pan with six paper muffin cases.

2 Roughly crush the sugar cubes and put to one side. Sift together the flour, baking powder and salt.

3 In a large bowl, combine the beaten egg, caster sugar, melted butter, vanilla extract and milk.

4 Fold in the sifted flour and spoon the mixture into the muffin cases. Sprinkle with the brown sugar. Bake for 30–35 minutes. Cool on a wire rack.

EASY		NUTRITIONAL INFORMATION		Makes
Preparation Time 10 minutes	**Cooking Time** 30–35 minutes, plus cooling	**Per Muffin** 233 calories, 8g fat (of which 5g saturates), 38g carbohydrate, 0.4g salt	Vegetarian	**6**

Lamingtons

125g (4oz) unsalted butter, softened, plus extra to grease

125g (4oz) golden caster sugar

2 medium eggs

125g (4oz) self-raising flour, sifted

1 tsp baking powder

2 tsp vanilla extract

For the topping

200g (7oz) icing sugar

50g (2oz) cocoa powder

25g (1oz) unsalted butter, cubed

5 tbsp milk

200g (7oz) desiccated coconut

1 Preheat the oven to 180°C (160°C fan oven) mark 4. Grease and line a 15cm (6in) square cake tin.

2 Put the butter, caster sugar, eggs, flour, baking powder and vanilla extract into a bowl and beat with an electric whisk until creamy. Turn the mixture into the prepared tin and level the surface. Bake for about 30 minutes until just firm to the touch and a skewer inserted into the centre comes out clean. Transfer to a wire rack to cool. Wrap and store, preferably overnight, so that the cake is easier to slice.

3 To make the topping, sift the icing sugar and cocoa powder into a bowl. Put the butter and milk into a small pan and heat until the butter has just melted. Pour over the icing sugar and stir until smooth, adding 2–3 tbsp water so that the icing thickly coats the back of a spoon.

4 Trim the side crusts from the cake and cut into 16 squares. Place a sheet of greaseproof paper under a wire rack to catch the drips. Scatter the coconut on to a large plate. Pierce a piece of cake through the top crust and dip into the icing until coated, turning the cake gently. Transfer to the wire rack. Once you've coated half the pieces, roll them in the coconut and transfer to a plate. Repeat with the remainder and leave to set for a couple of hours before serving.

Cook's Tip

If towards the end of coating the chocolate topping mixture has thickened, thin it down with a drop of water and carefully stir in.

Makes 16	EASY		NUTRITIONAL INFORMATION	
	Preparation Time 40 minutes	**Cooking Time** 30 minutes, plus cooling and setting	**Per Cake** 273 calories, 17g fat (of which 12g saturates), 29g carbohydrate, 0.4g salt	Vegetarian

Try Something Different

Double Chocolate Chip Muffins: omit the blueberries and lemon zest. Replace 40g (1½oz) of the flour with cocoa powder, then add 150g (5oz) chopped dark chocolate into the dry ingredients in step 3.

Blueberry Muffins

2 medium eggs
250ml (9fl oz) semi-skimmed milk
250g (9oz) golden granulated sugar
2 tsp vanilla extract
350g (12oz) plain flour
4 tsp baking powder
250g (9oz) blueberries, frozen
finely grated zest of 2 lemons

1 Preheat the oven to 200°C (180°C fan oven) mark 6. Line a bun tin or muffin pan with 12 paper muffin cases.

2 Put the eggs, milk, sugar and vanilla extract into a bowl and mix well.

3 In another bowl, sift the flour and baking powder together, then add the blueberries and lemon zest. Toss together and then make a well in the centre.

4 Pour the egg mixture into the flour and blueberries, and mix in gently – overbeating will make the muffins tough.

5 Divide the mixture among the muffin cases and bake for 20–25 minutes. These are best eaten on the day they are made.

Makes 12	EASY		NUTRITIONAL INFORMATION	
	Preparation Time 10 minutes	**Cooking Time** 20–25 minutes, plus cooling	**Per Muffin** 218 calories, 2g fat (of which trace saturates), 49g carbohydrate, 0.5g salt	Vegetarian

Freezing Tip

To freeze Once the muffins are cold, pack, seal and freeze.
To use Thaw at cool room temperature or individually in
the microwave, allowing 30 seconds on full power.

Chocolate Banana Muffins

275g (10oz) self-raising flour

1 tsp bicarbonate of soda

$\frac{1}{2}$ tsp salt

3 large bananas, about 450g (1lb)

125g (4oz) golden caster sugar

1 large egg, beaten

50ml (2fl oz) semi-skimmed milk

75g (3oz) unsalted butter, melted and cooled

50g (2oz) plain chocolate, chopped

1. Preheat the oven to 180°C (160°C fan oven) mark 4.
Line a bun tin or muffin pan with 12 paper muffin
cases. Sift the flour, bicarbonate of soda and salt
together into a large mixing bowl and put to one
side.

2. Peel the bananas and mash with a fork in a bowl.
Add the caster sugar, egg, milk and melted butter,
and mix until well combined.

3. Add this to the flour mixture, with the chopped
chocolate. Stir gently, using only a few strokes, until
the flour is only just incorporated – do not overmix.
The mixture should be lumpy.

4. Spoon the mixture into the muffin cases, half-filling
them. Bake in the oven for 20 minutes or until the
muffins are well risen and golden. Transfer to a wire
rack to cool. Serve warm or cold.

EASY		NUTRITIONAL INFORMATION		Makes
Preparation Time 15 minutes	**Cooking Time** 20 minutes, plus cooling	**Per Muffin** 228 calories, 7g fat (of which 4g saturates), 40g carbohydrate, 0.5g salt	Vegetarian	**12**

Spiced Carrot Muffins

125g (4oz) unsalted butter, softened

125g (4oz) light muscovado sugar

3 pieces of preserved stem ginger, drained and chopped

150g (5oz) self-raising flour, sifted

1½ tsp baking powder

1 tbsp ground mixed spice

25g (1oz) ground almonds

3 medium eggs

finely grated zest of ½ orange

150g (5oz) carrots, grated

50g (2oz) pecan nuts, chopped

50g (2oz) sultanas

3 tbsp white rum or orange liqueur (optional)

For the icing

200g (7oz) full-fat cream cheese

75g (3oz) icing sugar

1 tsp lemon juice

12 unsprayed rose petals to decorate (optional)

1 Preheat the oven to 180°C (160°C fan oven) mark 4. Line a bun tin or muffin pan with 12 paper muffin cases.

2 Beat together the butter, muscovado sugar and stem ginger until pale and creamy.

3 Add the flour, baking powder, spice, ground almonds, eggs and orange zest. Beat well until combined.

4 Stir in the carrots, pecan nuts and sultanas. Divide the mixture among the muffin cases and bake for about 20–25 minutes until risen and just firm. A skewer inserted into the centre should come out clean. Transfer to a wire rack and leave to cool.

5 To make the icing, beat the cream cheese in a bowl until softened. Beat in the icing sugar and lemon juice to give a smooth icing that just holds its shape.

6 Drizzle each cake with a little liqueur, if using. Use a small palette knife to spread a little icing over each cake. Decorate each with a petal, if you like.

EASY		NUTRITIONAL INFORMATION		Makes
Preparation Time 30 minutes	**Cooking Time** 20–25 minutes, plus cooling	**Per Muffin** 333 calories, 22g fat (of which 11g saturates), 31g carbohydrate, 0.5g salt	Vegetarian	**12**

butter to grease (optional)

50g (2oz) raisins

finely grated zest and juice of 1 orange

125g (4oz) wholemeal flour

25g (1oz) wheatgerm

3 tbsp caster sugar

2 tsp baking powder

a pinch of salt

1 large medium egg, beaten

50ml (2fl oz) milk

50ml (2fl oz) sunflower oil

2 medium-sized ripe bananas, about 225g (8oz) when peeled, roughly mashed

Wholemeal Banana Muffins

For the topping

5 tbsp orange marmalade

50g (2oz) banana chips, roughly chopped

50g (2oz) walnuts, roughly chopped

1 Preheat the oven to 200°C (180°C fan oven) mark 6. Line a bun tin or muffin pan with six paper muffin cases. Put the raisins in a bowl, pour the orange juice over and leave to soak for 1 hour.

2 Put the orange zest in a bowl with the flour, wheatgerm, sugar, baking powder and salt, and mix together. Make a well in the centre.

3 In a separate bowl, mix the egg, milk and oil, then pour into the flour mixture and stir until just blended. Drain the raisins, reserving 1 tbsp juice, and stir into the mixture with the bananas. Don't overmix. Fill each muffin case two-thirds full. Bake for 20–25 minutes until a skewer inserted into the centre comes out clean. Transfer to a wire rack to cool slightly.

4 For the topping, gently heat the marmalade with the reserved orange juice until melted. Simmer for 1 minute, then add the banana chips and walnuts. Spoon on top of the muffins. Serve while still warm.

Makes 6	EASY		NUTRITIONAL INFORMATION	
	Preparation Time 15 minutes, plus 1 hour soaking	**Cooking Time** 20–25 minutes	**Per Muffin** 341 calories, 13g fat (of which 2g saturates), 51g carbohydrate, 0.6g salt	Vegetarian

Bran and Apple Muffins

250ml (9fl oz) semi-skimmed milk
2 tbsp orange juice
50g (2oz) All Bran
9 ready-to-eat prunes
100g (3½oz) light muscovado sugar
2 medium egg whites
1 tbsp golden syrup
150g (5oz) plain flour, sifted
1 tsp baking powder
1 tsp ground cinnamon
1 eating apple, peeled and grated
demerara sugar to sprinkle

1 Preheat the oven to 190°C (170°C fan oven) mark 5. Line a bun tin or muffin pan with ten paper muffin cases.

2 In a bowl, mix the milk and orange juice with the All Bran. Put to one side for 10 minutes.

3 Put the prunes in a food processor or blender with 100ml (3½fl oz) water and whiz for 2–3 minutes to make a purée, then add the muscovado sugar and whiz briefly to mix.

4 In a grease-free bowl, whisk the egg whites until they form soft peaks, Add the whites to the milk mixture with the golden syrup, flour, baking powder, cinnamon, grated apple and prune mixture. Fold all the ingredients together gently.

5 Spoon the mixture into the muffin cases and bake for 30 minutes or until well risen and golden brown. Sprinkle with demerara sugar just before serving.

EASY		**NUTRITIONAL INFORMATION**		Makes
Preparation Time 20 minutes	**Cooking Time** 30 minutes	**Per Muffin** 137 calories, 1g fat (of which trace saturates), 31g carbohydrate, 0.3g salt	Vegetarian	**10**

4

Simple Cakes and Teabreads

225g (8oz) unsalted butter, softened, plus extra to grease
grated zest of 2 lemons and 2 tbsp lemon juice
225g (8oz) caster sugar
4 large eggs, beaten
75g (3oz) candied lemon peel, finely chopped (optional)
225g (8oz) self-raising flour, sifted

Warm Lemon Syrup Cake

For the syrup and topping
175g (6oz) caster sugar
finely sliced zest and strained juice of 3 lemons
75ml (2½fl oz) water

1 Preheat the oven to 180°C (160°C fan oven) mark 4. Grease and baseline a 20.5cm (8in) round deep cake tin.

2 Cream together the butter and lemon zest. Gradually beat in the sugar, followed by the eggs; the mixture should be stiff. Fold in the flour, candied peel, if using, and lemon juice. Spoon the mixture into the prepared tin and bake for about 1 hour or until golden.

3 Meanwhile, prepare the syrup and topping. Put the sugar, lemon juice and water into a pan. Warm gently until the sugar dissolves, then bring to the boil and bubble for 1 minute. Cool.

4 As soon as the cake is cooked, turn out into a shallow dish and immediately spoon over the syrup. Leave for about 30 minutes for the syrup to soak in. Serve warm, topped with the sliced lemon zest.

Serves	EASY		NUTRITIONAL INFORMATION	
12	**Preparation Time** 15 minutes	**Cooking Time** 1 hour, plus cooling	**Per Serving** 360 calories, 18g fat (of which 10g saturates), 49g carbohydrate, 0.5g salt	Vegetarian

Lime Drizzle Loaf

175g (6oz) self-raising flour, sifted with a pinch of salt

175g (6oz) unsalted butter, diced

175g (6oz) golden caster sugar

3 medium eggs, beaten

50g (2oz) sweetened and tenderised coconut

grated zest and juice of 2 limes

1 tsp baking powder

For the icing

1 lime

125g (4oz) golden icing sugar, sifted

1 tbsp sweetened and tenderised coconut to decorate

1 Preheat the oven to 180°C (160°C fan oven) mark 4. Line a 900g (2lb) loaf tin.

2 Put the flour, salt, butter, caster sugar, eggs, coconut, lime zest and juice and baking powder in the bowl of a mixer, fitted with a K beater. Mix together slowly, gradually increasing the speed and mixing for 2 minutes. (Alternatively, use a hand mixer.)

3 Pour the mixture (it'll be quite runny) into the tin and bake for 45–55 minutes until golden, well risen and cooked through – a skewer inserted into the centre should come out clean. Leave to cool for 10 minutes, then lift out the cake, keeping it in the paper.

4 To make the icing, finely grate the zest from the lime and cut away the white pith. Chop the lime flesh, then put in a mini processor or blender with the zest and whiz for 1–2 minutes until finely chopped. Add the icing sugar and blend until smooth. Pour over the cake, then sprinkle the coconut on top to decorate.

EASY		**NUTRITIONAL INFORMATION**		**Serves**
Preparation Time 15 minutes	**Cooking Time** 45–55 minutes, plus cooling	**Per Serving** 306 calories, 17g fat (of which 11g saturates), 38g carbohydrate, 0.4g salt	Vegetarian	**12**

Victoria Sponge

250g (9oz) unsalted butter, softened, plus extra to grease

250g (9oz) golden caster sugar

5 medium eggs

250g (9oz) self-raising flour

For the filling

200g (7oz) mascarpone cheese

7 tbsp strawberry conserve

For the decoration

250g (9oz) icing sugar

1 tsp rosewater

a few drops of pink food colouring

1 Preheat the oven to 190°C (170°C fan oven) mark 5. Grease and baseline two 20.5cm (8in) sandwich tins.

2 Put the butter and caster sugar in a large bowl and cream together using an electric whisk until the mixture is pale and fluffy. Add three of the eggs, one at a time, whisking well between each addition.

3 Add 4 tbsp of the flour (to stop the mixture curdling), then whisk in the remaining eggs, one at a time, and continue to whisk. Sift the remaining flour into the bowl and fold gently into the mixture using a large spoon. The mixture should be smooth and have a dropping consistency.

4 Divide the mixture between the prepared tins and level the surface. Bake for 25–30 minutes until golden, springy to the touch and shrinking away from the sides of the tins.

5 Leave to cool in the tins for 5 minutes, then turn on to a wire rack and remove the lining paper. When cold, spread one cake with mascarpone. Spoon on the jam, then spread to the edges. Top with the other cake and press down lightly.

6 To decorate, sift the icing sugar into a bowl, then add the rosewater, pink food colouring and 2–2½ tbsp hot water to create a smooth dropping consistency. Pour the icing on top of the cake, spreading it to the edge so that it drizzles down the side.

Try Something Different

Orange Victoria Sponge: fill with orange buttercream and top with orange icing. For the buttercream, cream together 75g (3oz) softened unsalted butter, 175g (6oz) sifted icing sugar, a little grated orange zest and 1-2 tbsp orange juice. For the icing, replace the rosewater with orange juice and omit the food colouring.

EASY		NUTRITIONAL INFORMATION		Serves
Preparation Time 30 minutes	**Cooking Time** 25–30 minutes, plus cooling	**Per Serving** 471 calories, 22g fat (of which 13g saturates), 66g carbohydrate, 0.6g salt	Vegetarian	12

Cook's Tip

To save time, you can microwave the orange. Put it in a small bowl, cover with 100ml (3½fl oz) water and cook in a 900W microwave oven on full power for 10–12 minutes until soft.

Almond and Orange Torte

oil to grease

flour to dust

1 medium orange

3 medium eggs

225g (8oz) golden caster sugar

250g (9oz) ground almonds

½ tsp baking powder

icing sugar to dust

crème fraîche to serve

1 Grease and line, then oil and flour a 20.5cm (8in) springform cake tin. Put the whole orange in a small pan and cover with water. Bring to the boil, then cover and simmer for at least 1 hour until tender (see Cook's Tip). Remove from the water and cool.

2 Cut the orange in half and remove the pips. Whiz in a food processor or blender to make a smooth purée.

3 Preheat the oven to 180°C (160°C fan oven) mark 4. Put the eggs and caster sugar in a bowl and whisk together until thick and pale. Fold in the almonds, baking powder and orange purée.

4 Pour the mixture into the prepared tin. Bake for 40–50 minutes until a skewer inserted into the centre comes out clean. Leave to cool in the tin.

5 Release the clasp on the tin and remove the cake. Carefully peel off the lining paper and put the cake on a serving plate. Dust with icing sugar, then cut into 12 wedges. Serve with crème fraîche.

Serves 12	EASY		NUTRITIONAL INFORMATION	
	Preparation Time 30 minutes	**Cooking Time** 1 hour 50 minutes, plus cooling	**Per Serving** 223 calories, 13g fat (of which 1g saturates), 22g carbohydrate, 0.1g salt	Vegetarian

175g (6oz) unsalted butter, softened, plus extra to grease

175g (6oz) plain flour

2 tsp baking powder

a pinch of salt

175g (6oz) caster sugar, plus extra to dust

$\frac{1}{2}$ tsp vanilla extract

grated zest of 1 lemon

3 medium eggs, beaten

milk

225g (8oz) small fresh cherries, stoned

Fresh Cherry Cake

1 Preheat the oven to 190°C (170°C fan oven) mark 5. Grease and baseline a 900g (2lb) loaf tin.

2 Sift the flour with the baking powder and salt. Cream together the butter and sugar until pale and fluffy. Gradually beat in the vanilla extract, lemon zest and eggs. Gently fold in the flour. If the mixture seems a little stiff, add a small amount of milk. Fold in the stoned cherries.

3 Turn the mixture into the prepared tin and bake for about 1 hour 10 minutes or until risen, well browned and slightly shrunk away from the sides of the tin. Cover lightly with foil, if necessary, to prevent overbrowning.

4 Leave to cool in the tin for about 10 minutes, then turn out on to a wire rack to cool completely. Store wrapped, in the refrigerator. Dust with caster sugar and cut into slices to serve.

EASY		NUTRITIONAL INFORMATION		Serves
Preparation Time 10 minutes	**Cooking Time** 1 hour 10 minutes, plus cooling	**Per Serving** 367 calories, 20g fat (of which 12g saturates), 44g carbohydrate, 0.8g salt	Vegetarian	**8**

Blackberry and Cinnamon Yogurt Loaf

125ml (4fl oz) sunflower oil, plus extra to grease
175g (6oz) plain flour
1½ tsp baking powder
1½ tsp ground cinnamon
200g (7oz) frozen blackberries
125g (4oz) golden caster sugar
grated zest and juice of 1 lemon
125ml (4fl oz) Greek yogurt
3 medium eggs, beaten
icing sugar to dust

1 Preheat the oven to 190°C (170°C fan oven) mark 5. Grease and baseline a 900g (2lb) loaf tin.

2 Sift the flour, baking powder and cinnamon into a bowl, add the frozen berries and toss to coat. Make a well in the centre.

3 In another bowl, whisk together the caster sugar, oil, lemon zest and juice, yogurt and eggs. Pour into the well in the flour mixture and stir.

4 Spoon the mixture into the prepared tin, level the surface and bake for 55 minutes (cover lightly with foil if the top is browning too quickly) or until a skewer inserted into the centre comes out clean. Leave in the tin to cool. Remove from the tin and dust with icing sugar.

Try Something Different

Apple and Cinnamon Yogurt Loaf: replace the blackberries with 2 small Cox's or Braeburn apples, peeled, cored and chopped.

Raspberry and White Chocolate Yogurt Loaf: omit the ground cinnamon. Replace the blackberries with 125g (4oz) frozen raspberries and 75g (3oz) chopped white chocolate, and use orange zest and juice instead of lemon.

Serves 8	EASY		NUTRITIONAL INFORMATION	
	Preparation Time 15 minutes	**Cooking Time** 55 minutes, plus cooling	**Per Serving** 287 calories, 15g fat (of which 3g saturates), 35g carbohydrate, 0.1g salt	Vegetarian

Pineapple and Coconut Loaf

125g (4oz) unsalted butter, softened, plus extra to grease

150g (5oz) wholemeal flour, sifted

125g (4oz) dark muscovado sugar

2 medium eggs

2 tsp baking powder

¼ tsp mixed spice

50g (2oz) desiccated coconut, plus extra to decorate

400g can pineapple in natural juice,
drained and roughly chopped

icing sugar to decorate

1 Preheat the oven to 180°C (160°C fan oven) mark 4. Grease and baseline a 450g (1lb) loaf tin.

2 Put the flour and muscovado sugar in a food processor and whiz for 1–2 minutes until well mixed. (Alternatively, put into a bowl and stir until the sugar is well combined with the flour, breaking down any lumps with a wooden spoon.) Add the remaining ingredients and mix until smooth.

3 Turn the mixture into the prepared tin, level the surface and brush lightly with 2 tbsp cold water. Bake for 50 minutes or until a skewer inserted into the centre comes out clean (if necessary, cover lightly with foil after 40 minutes to prevent overbrowning).

4 Leave in the tin for 10 minutes, then transfer to a wire rack to cool completely. Decorate with a little desiccated coconut and icing sugar.

Serves 10	EASY		NUTRITIONAL INFORMATION	
	Preparation Time 20 minutes	**Cooking Time** 50 minutes, plus cooling	**Per Serving** 254 calories, 15g fat (of which 10g saturates), 28g carbohydrate, 0.2g salt	Vegetarian

125g (4oz) unsalted butter, diced, plus extra to grease
225g (8oz) self-raising flour, sifted
½ tsp salt
175g (6oz) granulated sugar, golden if possible
2 large eggs, beaten
2 large Granny Smith apples, peeled, cored and sliced
150g (5oz) blueberries
175g (6oz) apricot jam
1 tbsp lemon juice

Apple and Blueberry Cake

1 Preheat the oven to 190°C (170°C fan oven) mark 5. Grease and baseline a 20.5cm (8in) springform tin with non-stick baking parchment. Put the flour and salt in a large mixing bowl, add the diced butter and rub in the flour until the mixture looks like fine breadcrumbs. Add 150g (5oz) sugar with the beaten eggs and stir well.

2 Spread half the mixture in a thin layer in the tin, then layer the sliced apples and the blueberries evenly over the surface, setting aside a little of the fruit for the top of the cake. Sprinkle with the remaining sugar, then spoon in the rest of the cake mixture. Add the remaining apple slices and blueberries, pressing them down slightly into the mixture.

3 Bake for 45–55 minutes until risen and firm to the touch – a skewer inserted into the centre of the cake should come out clean. Cool in the tin for 10 minutes, then turn out on to a wire rack to cool.

4 Warm the jam and lemon juice in a small pan until evenly combined. Sieve the mixture and, while it's still warm, brush it over the top of the cake. Serve immediately.

Freezing Tip

To freeze Wrap the cake in a freezer bag and freeze for up to one month.
To use Thaw at cool room temperature for 3 hours. Slice and heat individual slices in the microwave on full power for 1 minute per slice.

EASY		NUTRITIONAL INFORMATION		Serves
Preparation Time 20 minutes, plus cooling	**Cooking Time** 1 hour, plus cooling	**Per Serving** 380 calories, 15g fat (of which 9g saturates), 62g carbohydrate, 0.9g salt	Vegetarian	**8**

Apricot and Almond Traybake

250g (9oz) unsalted butter, softened, plus extra to grease

225g (8oz) golden caster sugar

275g (10oz) self-raising flour, sifted

2 tsp baking powder

finely grated zest of 1 orange and 2 tbsp orange juice

75g (3oz) ground almonds

5 medium eggs, lightly beaten

225g (8oz) ready-to-eat dried apricots, roughly chopped

25g (1oz) flaked almonds

icing sugar to dust (optional)

1 Preheat the oven to 180°C (160°C fan oven) mark 4. Grease and baseline a 33 x 20.5cm (13 x 8in) tin.

2 Put the butter, caster sugar, flour, baking powder, orange zest, ground almonds and eggs into the bowl of a large freestanding mixer. Mix on a low setting for 30 seconds, then increase the speed and mix for 1 minute until thoroughly combined. (Alternatively, mix well using a wooden spoon.)

3 Remove the bowl from the mixer. Fold in the apricots with a large metal spoon. Spoon the mixture into the prepared tin, then smooth the surface with a palette knife and sprinkle the flaked almonds over the top.

4 Bake for 30–40 minutes until risen and golden brown. It's ready when a skewer inserted into the centre comes out clean.

5 Leave to cool in the tin, then cut into 18 bars. Dust with icing sugar, if you like.

EASY		NUTRITIONAL INFORMATION		Makes
Preparation Time 20 minutes	**Cooking Time** 30–40 minutes, plus cooling	**Per Bar** 277 calories, 16g fat (of which 8g saturates), 30g carbohydrate, 0.4g salt	Vegetarian Gluten free • Dairy free	**18**

30-minute Fruit Cake

125g (4oz) unsalted butter, softened
125g (4oz) light muscovado sugar
grated zest of 1 lemon
2 medium eggs
a few drops of vanilla extract
150g (5oz) self-raising flour, sifted
1 tsp baking powder
a little lemon juice, as needed
50g (2oz) glacé cherries, chopped
175g (6oz) mixed dried fruit
25g (1oz) desiccated coconut
25g (1oz) demerara sugar
50g (2oz) flaked almonds

1   Preheat the oven to 190°C (170°C fan oven) mark 5. Grease and baseline a 28 x 18cm (11 x 7in) shallow baking tin.

2   Beat together the butter, muscovado sugar, lemon zest, eggs, vanilla extract, flour and baking powder. Add a little lemon juice, if necessary, to form a soft dropping consistency. Stir in the cherries, dried fruit and coconut.

3   Spoon the mixture into the prepared tin, level the surface and sprinkle with demerara sugar and almonds. Bake for 30 minutes or until golden.

4   Cool in the tin for a few minutes, then turn out on to a wire rack to cool completely.

Serves 18	EASY		NUTRITIONAL INFORMATION	
	Preparation Time 15 minutes	Cooking Time 30 minutes, plus cooling	Per Serving 180 calories, 9g fat (of which 5g saturates), 24g carbohydrate, 0.2g salt	Vegetarian

Freezing Tip

To freeze Complete to the end of step 3, wrap the cake in clingfilm and foil. Freeze for up to one month.
To use Thaw for 3 hours and complete the cake.

100g (3½oz) unsalted butter, diced, plus extra to grease

100g (3½oz) soft brown sugar

3 tbsp black treacle

100ml (3½fl oz) milk

2 tbsp brandy

1 large egg, beaten

150g (5oz) plain flour

2 tsp ground ginger

2 tsp ground cinnamon

1 tsp bicarbonate of soda

75g (3oz) ready-to-eat pitted prunes, chopped coarsely

Sticky Ginger Ring

For the topping

225g (8oz) golden icing sugar, sifted

2 pieces preserved stem ginger, drained and roughly chopped

1 Preheat the oven to 150°C (130°C fan oven) mark 2. Generously grease a 20.5cm (8in), 600ml (1 pint) capacity round ring mould. Put the butter, brown sugar and treacle in a pan and heat gently until melted, stirring all the time. Add the milk and brandy. Cool, then beat in the egg.

2 Sift the flour, spices and bicarbonate of soda into a large mixing bowl. Make a well in the centre, pour in the treacle mixture and stir together until all the flour has been combined – it should have a soft dropping consistency. Stir in the chopped prunes.

3 Pour the mixture into the greased mould and bake for 1 hour or until firm to the touch and a skewer inserted in the centre comes out clean. Leave in the tin for 10 minutes, then turn out on to a wire rack.

4 To make the topping, mix the icing sugar with about 2 tbsp hot water to create a coating consistency. Drizzle over the cake, then decorate with stem ginger.

EASY		NUTRITIONAL INFORMATION		Serves 8
Preparation Time 15 minutes, plus cooling	**Cooking Time** 1 hour	**Per Serving** 375 calories, 12g fat (of which 7g saturates), 64g carbohydrate, 0.3g salt	Vegetarian	

Get Ahead

Complete the recipe up to the end of step 6. Wrap the cake in foil and store in an airtight container for up to five days.

Celebration Chocolate Cake

butter or sunflower oil to grease

200g (7oz) plain chocolate (at least 50% cocoa solids), broken into pieces

5 large eggs

125g (4oz) golden caster sugar

100g (3½oz) ground almonds

1 tbsp coffee liqueur, such as Tia Maria

fresh raspberries to decorate

icing sugar to dust

1 Grease a 12.5cm (5in) deep round cake tin and line with greaseproof paper, making sure the paper comes 5-7.5cm (2–3in) above the tin.

2 Melt the chocolate in a heatproof bowl over a pan of gently simmering water. Remove the bowl from the pan and leave to cool slightly. Meanwhile, preheat the oven to 170°C (150°C fan oven) mark 3.

3 Separate all but one of the eggs, putting the whites to one side. Put the yolks, the whole egg and the sugar in the bowl of a freestanding mixer, or use an electric whisk. Whisk at high speed for 5 minutes or until the mixture is pale and leaves a ribbon trail.

4 Set the mixer to a very low speed, add the chocolate and then the almonds, and mix until evenly combined. Put to one side.

5 Whisk the egg whites until they form soft peaks. Beat one quarter of the egg whites into the chocolate mixture to loosen, then fold in the rest.

6 Pour the mixture into the prepared tin. Bake for 1–1¼ hours until a skewer inserted into the centre of the cake for 30 seconds comes out hot. Make several holes in the cake with the skewer, then pour over the liqueur. Leave in the tin for 30 minutes, then turn out on to a wire rack and leave until cold.

7 Transfer to a plate, spoon raspberries on top and tie a ribbon around the cake. Dust with icing sugar.

Serves 16	EASY		NUTRITIONAL INFORMATION	
	Preparation Time 40 minutes	**Cooking Time** 1–1¼ hours, plus cooling	**Per Serving** 161 calories, 9g fat (of which 3g saturates), 17g carbohydrate, 0.1g salt	Vegetarian Gluten free • Dairy free

butter to grease

175g (6oz) plain flour, sifted

2 tsp baking powder

½ tsp bicarbonate of soda

½ tsp salt

175g (6oz) light muscovado sugar

2 large eggs

3 medium ripe bananas, mashed

150g (5oz) natural yogurt

150g (5oz) butterscotch chocolate or milk chocolate, roughly chopped

100g (3½oz) pecan nuts, chopped

1–2 tbsp demerara sugar

Banana and Chocolate Loaf

1 Preheat the oven to 170°C (150°C fan oven) mark 3. Grease and line a 1.4kg (3lb) loaf tin.

2 Put the flour, baking powder, bicarbonate of soda and salt in a large bowl and mix together.

3 In a separate bowl, beat together the muscovado sugar and eggs with an electric hand whisk until pale and fluffy. Carefully stir in the bananas, yogurt, chocolate and 50g (2oz) pecan nuts, followed by the flour mixture.

4 Spoon the mixture into the prepared tin and sprinkle over the remaining chopped pecan nuts and the demerara sugar. Bake for 1 hour or until a skewer inserted into the centre comes out clean. Leave to cool in the tin, then turn out and slice.

Serves 15	EASY		NUTRITIONAL INFORMATION	
	Preparation Time 20 minutes	**Cooking Time** 1 hour, plus cooling	**Per Serving** 221 calories, 9g fat (of which 2g saturates), 34g carbohydrate, 0.2g salt	Vegetarian

Carrot Traybake

100g (3½oz) unsalted butter, chopped, plus extra to grease

150g (5oz) carrots, grated

100g (3½oz) each sultanas and chopped dried dates

50g (2oz) tenderised coconut

1 tsp ground cinnamon and ½ tsp freshly grated nutmeg

330g bottle maple syrup

150ml (¼ pint) apple juice

grated zest and juice of 2 oranges

225g (8oz) wholemeal self-raising flour, sifted

2 tsp bicarbonate of soda

125g (4oz) walnut pieces

For the topping

pared zest from ½–1 orange

200g (7oz) each cream cheese and crème fraîche

2 tbsp icing sugar

1 tsp vanilla extract

1 Preheat the oven to 190°C (170°C fan oven) mark 5. Grease and line a 23cm (9in) square cake tin.

2 Put the butter, carrots, sultanas, dates, coconut, spices, maple syrup, apple juice and orange zest and juice into a large pan. Cover and bring to the boil, then cook for 5 minutes. Tip into a bowl and leave to cool.

3 Put the flour, bicarbonate of soda and walnuts in a large bowl and stir together. Add the cooled carrot mixture and stir well.

4 Spoon the mixture into the prepared tin and bake for 45 minutes–1 hour until firm. Leave in the tin for 10 minutes, then transfer to a wire rack to cool completely.

5 To make the topping, finely slice the orange zest. Put the cream cheese, crème fraîche, icing sugar and vanilla extract in a bowl and stir with a spatula until well combined. Spread over the cake, cut into 16 squares, then top with the zest.

EASY		NUTRITIONAL INFORMATION		Makes
Preparation Time 30 minutes, plus cooling	**Cooking Time** 50 minutes–1 hour 5 minutes, plus cooling	**Per Serving** 399 calories, 25g fat (of which 13g saturates), 41g carbohydrate, 0.4g salt	Vegetarian	**16**

Sweet Cherry Bread

oil to grease

350g (12oz) strong white bread flour, plus extra to dust

½ tsp salt

2 tsp ground mixed spice

1 tbsp cinnamon

25g (1oz) caster sugar

15g (½oz) fast-action dried yeast

75g (3oz) unsalted butter, diced

200ml (7fl oz) milk, warmed

125g (4oz) white almond paste, roughly chopped

125g (4oz) glacé cherries

3 tbsp honey, warmed

75g (3oz) icing sugar, sifted

1 Grease and baseline a 20.5cm (8in) round deep cake tin. Sift the flour, salt, spices and caster sugar into a bowl. Add the yeast. Rub in the butter. Add the milk to make a dough (if the dough is too dry, add a little more milk). Turn out on to a lightly floured surface and knead for 10 minutes. Put the dough in a lightly oiled bowl, cover with oiled clingfilm and leave in a warm place for 2 hours or until doubled in size.

2 Turn out the dough on to a lightly floured surface and knead lightly. Shape into an oval, 60cm (24in) long. Scatter the almond paste and cherries over the surface and roll the dough up lengthways, then form a tight coil. Put in the cake tin, cover and leave in a warm place for 30 minutes or until doubled in size. Preheat the oven to 180°C (160°C fan oven) mark 4.

3 Bake for 40 minutes or until golden; it should sound hollow when tapped underneath. Cool on a wire rack. When cool, brush with honey. Mix the icing sugar with a few drops of water and drizzle over the bread. Store in an airtight container for up to two days.

Serves 8	A LITTLE EFFORT		NUTRITIONAL INFORMATION	
	Preparation Time 40 minutes, plus 2½ hours rising	**Cooking Time** 40 minutes, plus cooling	**Per Serving** 310 calories, 4g fat (of which trace saturates), 66g carbohydrate, 0.4g salt	Vegetarian

Cook's Tips

This cake is made with yeast, so it's best eaten within two days, before it goes stale. If you have any left over, wrap and freeze in slices – it's tasty toasted or used for making bread and butter pudding.

If you don't have a mixer with a beater attachment, use a food processor with a flat plastic blade.

2 tsp fast-action dried yeast

300g (11oz) plain white flour, plus extra to dust

4 large eggs

100ml (3½fl oz) milk

225g (8oz) unsalted butter, softened, plus extra to grease

75g (3oz) caster sugar

pinch of salt

grated zest of 1 lemon

100g (3½oz) split blanched almonds, lightly toasted

200g (7oz) raisins, soaked overnight in 3 tbsp light rum

whole glacé fruits and nuts to decorate

icing sugar to dust

Kugelhopf

1 Put the yeast and flour in a food mixer. Lightly whisk the eggs and milk then, with the machine running on a slow speed, pour on to the flour and mix for 10 minutes or until the dough is smooth, shiny and elastic. In another bowl, beat the butter, caster sugar, salt and lemon zest then, with the mixer running, add to the dough, a spoonful at a time, until evenly incorporated. Turn the mixture into a large, lightly floured bowl. Cover with clingfilm and chill overnight.

2 Generously butter a 2 litre (3½ pint) kugelhopf mould. Press a few almonds on to the sides of the mould. Chill. Roughly chop the remaining almonds. Mix into the dough with the raisins and rum, then put in the mould, cover and leave for 3 hours in a warm place until it has risen nearly to the top of the mould. Preheat the oven to 200°C (180°C fan oven) mark 6. Bake for 10 minutes. Cover with greaseproof paper, reduce the temperature to 190°C (170°C fan oven) mark 5 and bake for 40–45 minutes until the kugelhopf sounds hollow when you tap the mould. Cool in the tin for 15 minutes. Turn on to a wire rack to cool completely. Decorate with glacé fruits and nuts and serve dusted with icing sugar.

A LITTLE EFFORT		NUTRITIONAL INFORMATION		Serves
Preparation Time 45 minutes, plus overnight chilling and 3 hours rising	**Cooking Time** 50–55 minutes, plus cooling	**Per Serving** 382 calories, 22g fat (of which 11g saturates), 39g carbohydrate, 0.4g salt	Vegetarian	**12**

5

Rich Cakes and Gateaux

Cook's Tips

Ginger and Whisky Sauce: gently heat 300ml (½ pint) single cream with 2 tsp preserved stem ginger syrup and 1 tsp whisky. Serve just warm, with the cake.
The cake may also be served with sliced oranges soaked in ginger syrup and Cointreau.

Warm Ginger Ricotta Cake

225g (8oz) digestive biscuits

75g (3oz) unsalted butter, melted, plus extra to grease

200g full-fat soft cheese

225g (8oz) ricotta cheese

4 tbsp double cream

3 medium eggs, separated

1 tbsp cornflour

1 piece of preserved stem ginger in syrup, finely chopped, plus 1 tbsp syrup

125g (4oz) icing sugar

Ginger and Whisky Sauce to serve (optional, see Cook's Tips)

1 Preheat the oven to 200°C (180°C fan oven) mark 6. Grease a 20.5cm (8in) springform cake tin. Put the biscuits in a food processor and whiz until finely ground. Add the melted butter and whiz for a further minute. Use just over half the crumb mixture to cover the base and sides of the cake tin. Put to one side.

2 Beat or whiz together the cheeses, cream, egg yolks, cornflour, ginger and syrup. Transfer to a large bowl.

3 Whisk the egg whites until they form soft peaks. Gradually whisk in the icing sugar, keeping the meringue very stiff and shiny. Fold into the ginger mixture and spoon on to the biscuit base. Sprinkle over the remaining biscuit crumbs.

4 Bake for 30 minutes. Reduce the oven temperature to 180°C (160°C fan oven) mark 4, cover the cake loosely with foil and bake for a further 45 minutes. The cake should be just set in the centre. Cool for 15 minutes on a wire rack. Serve warm, with Ginger and Whisky Sauce if you like.

Serves 8	EASY		NUTRITIONAL INFORMATION	
	Preparation Time 25 minutes	**Cooking Time** 1¼ hours, plus cooling	**Per Serving** 494 calories, 36g fat (of which 21g saturates), 38g carbohydrate, 0.8g salt	Vegetarian

275g (10oz) amaretti biscuits, ratafias or macaroons

75g (3oz) unsalted butter, melted

700g (1½lb) mascarpone or full-fat cream cheese (at room temperature)

150g (5oz) caster sugar

3 medium eggs, separated

25g (1oz) plain flour, sifted

3 tbsp dark rum

½ tsp vanilla extract

175g (6oz) plain chocolate (at least 50% cocoa solids)

1 tbsp finely ground coffee

3 tbsp Tia Maria or other coffee liqueur

Tiramisu Torte

1 Put the biscuits in a food processor and whiz until finely ground. Add the melted butter and stir until well mixed. Spoon into a 23cm (9in) springform cake tin. Using the back of a spoon, press evenly over the base and 4cm (1½in) up the sides to form a shell. Chill for at least 30 minutes or until firm.

2 Preheat the oven to 200°C (180°C fan oven) mark 6. Using a wooden spoon or an electric mixer, beat the cheese until smooth. Add the sugar and beat again until smooth, then beat in the egg yolks. Transfer half of the mixture to another bowl and stir in the flour, rum and vanilla extract.

3 Melt the chocolate in a heatproof bowl over a pan of gently simmering water. Cool slightly, then stir in the coffee and coffee liqueur. Stir into the remaining half of the cheese mixture.

4 In a clean, grease-free bowl, whisk the egg whites until they form soft peaks, then fold half the egg whites into each flavoured cheese mixture. Spoon alternate mounds of the two mixtures into the biscuit case until full. Using a knife, swirl them together for a marbled effect.

5 Bake for 45 minutes, covering with foil if it seems to be overbrowning. At this stage the torte will be soft in the middle. Leave in the switched-off oven with the door slightly ajar, to cool; it will firm up during this time. Chill for several hours.

EASY		NUTRITIONAL INFORMATION		Serves
Preparation Time 40 minutes, plus chilling	**Cooking Time** 45 minutes, plus cooling	**Per Serving** 682 calories, 50g fat (of which 30g saturates), 51g carbohydrate, 0.9g salt	Vegetarian	**10**

Creamy Coffee and Praline Gateau

50g (2oz) unsalted butter, melted, plus extra to grease

125g (4oz) plain flour, sifted, plus extra to dust

4 large eggs, separated

125g (4oz) caster sugar

1 tbsp coffee granules, dissolved in 2 tsp boiling water

For the praline

50g (2oz) whole blanched hazelnuts

150g (5oz) caster sugar

For the filling

500g (1lb 2oz) mascarpone cheese

250g (9oz) icing sugar, sifted

2 tbsp coffee granules, dissolved in 1 tbsp boiling water

1. Preheat the oven to 190°C (170°C fan oven) mark 5. Grease two 18cm (7in) loose-based sandwich tins. Dust lightly with flour and tip out the excess. Whisk the egg whites until they form soft peaks. Whisk in one egg yolk; repeat with the other three yolks. Add the sugar, 1 tbsp at a time, and continue to whisk. The mixture should be thick enough to leave a trail when the whisk is lifted. Fold half the flour into the mixture, using a metal spoon. Mix the coffee into the melted butter, then pour around the edge of the egg mixture. Add the remaining flour and gradually fold in. Divide the mixture between the prepared tins and bake for 25 minutes until risen and firm to the touch. Turn out on to a wire rack and leave to cool.

2. To make the praline, line a baking sheet with baking parchment and scatter over the nuts. Dissolve the sugar in a heavy-based pan over a low heat, shaking the pan once or twice to help it dissolve evenly. Cook until it forms a dark golden-brown caramel. Pour over the nuts and leave to cool.

3. To make the filling, put the mascarpone and icing sugar in a large bowl, add the coffee and mix with an electric hand whisk. Slice each cake in half horizontally. Put one layer on to a plate and spread with a quarter of the filling. Continue layering in this way, finishing with a layer of mascarpone filling.

4. Break the praline into two or three pieces and put into a plastic bag. With a rolling pin, smash into smaller pieces. Use to decorate the top of the cake.

FOR THE CONFIDENT COOK		NUTRITIONAL INFORMATION		Serves
Preparation Time 45 minutes	**Cooking Time** 25 minutes, plus cooling	**Per Serving** 548 calories, 21g fat (of which 10g saturates), 83g carbohydrate, 0.2g salt	Vegetarian	**8**

125g (4oz) unsalted butter, softened, plus extra to grease

225g (8oz) plain chocolate (at least 50% cocoa solids)

5 large eggs, separated

150g (5oz) caster sugar

milk or plain chocolate curls to decorate

For the mousse layer and icing

2 tsp powdered gelatine

400g (14oz) white chocolate

4 large eggs, separated

300ml (½ pint) double cream

White Chocolate Mousse Cake

1 Preheat the oven to 190°C (170°C fan oven) mark 5. Grease and line a 20.5cm (8in) springform cake tin.

2 Melt the plain chocolate in a heatproof bowl over a pan of gently simmering water. Remove the bowl from the pan and cool slightly.

3 Meanwhile, using an electric whisk, whisk the five egg yolks and the sugar together in a heatproof bowl set over a pan of hot water until thick and creamy. Beat in the butter, a little at a time, until smooth. Off the heat, beat in the melted chocolate. Whisk the egg whites until they form soft peaks, then gently fold into the chocolate mixture. Pour into the prepared tin, then tap the tin firmly on the worksurface to disperse any bubbles. Bake for 50–55 minutes until risen and firm, covering with foil halfway through cooking. Leave to cool in the tin for 1 hour.

4 To make the mousse layer, sprinkle the gelatine over 2 tbsp water in a small heatproof bowl and leave to soak for about 10 minutes. Melt 225g (8oz) white

chocolate as in step 2 and cool slightly. Beat the four egg yolks into the chocolate, followed by 150ml (¼ pint) cream. Put the bowl of gelatine over a pan of gently simmering water until the gelatine has dissolved. Whisk the egg whites until they form soft peaks. Stir the gelatine into the chocolate mixture. Stir in a spoonful of egg white to lighten it, then fold in the remainder.

5 Split the cake horizontally. Line the same tin with greaseproof paper and put one round of cake in the base, pressing lightly to fit. Pour over the mousse, then chill for about 30 minutes. Put the remaining cake round on top and chill overnight.

6 To make the icing, put the remaining white chocolate in a bowl with the remaining cream and melt over a pan of gently simmering water until smooth. Cool slightly, beating the mixture until it thickens. Carefully remove the cake from the tin, gently easing away the parchment, and spread over the icing. Chill to set. Decorate with milk or dark chocolate curls.

Serves 16	FOR THE CONFIDENT COOK		NUTRITIONAL INFORMATION	
	Preparation Time 45 minutes, plus chilling	**Cooking Time** about 1 hour, plus cooling	**Per Serving** 433 calories, 31g fat (of which 18g saturates), 34g carbohydrate, 0.3g salt	Gluten free

Cook's Tip

Ganache: put 175g (6oz) broken-up plain chocolate, 75g (3oz) softened unsalted butter and 4 tbsp double cream into a heatproof bowl over a pan of gently simmering water. Leave to melt, then stir until smooth.

Decadent Chocolate Cake

225g (8oz) unsalted butter, softened, plus extra to grease

300g (11oz) plain chocolate (at least 70% cocoa solids), broken into pieces

225g (8oz) golden caster sugar

225g (8oz) ground almonds

8 large eggs, separated

125g (4oz) fresh brown breadcrumbs

ganache to cover (see Cook's Tip)

1 Preheat the oven to 180°C (160°C fan oven) mark 4. Grease and line a 23cm (9in) springform cake tin.

2 Melt the chocolate in a heatproof bowl over a pan of gently simmering water. Remove the bowl from the pan. Put the butter and sugar into a large bowl and beat together until light and creamy. Add the ground almonds, egg yolks and breadcrumbs, and beat well. Slowly add the melted chocolate and carefully stir it in, taking care not to overmix, as the chocolate may seize up. Put the egg whites into a clean, grease-free bowl and whisk until they form soft peaks. Add half the whites to the chocolate mixture and fold in lightly using a large metal spoon, then carefully fold in the remainder. Pour the mixture into the prepared tin and level the surface. Bake for 1 hour 20 minutes or until a skewer inserted into the centre comes out clean. Leave in the tin for 5 minutes, then transfer to a wire rack for 2–3 hours to cool completely.

3 Pour the ganache over the centre of the cake and spread it with a palette knife. Leave to set.

A LITTLE EFFORT		NUTRITIONAL INFORMATION		Serves
Preparation Time 30 minutes	**Cooking Time** 1½ hours, plus cooling	**Per Serving** 693 calories, 49g fat (of which 23g saturates), 54g carbohydrate, 0.7g salt	Vegetarian	**12**

Marshmallow Meringue Cake

225g (8oz) golden caster sugar
125g (4oz) light muscovado sugar
6 large eggs, separated
1 tsp cornflour
1/2 tsp vinegar
50g (2oz) flaked almonds, toasted (optional)
chocolate shavings and icing sugar to dust

For the filling

Marshmallow Ice Cream (see Cook's Tip)
4 bananas, about 450g (1lb)

Cook's Tip

Marshmallow Ice Cream: bring 450ml (3/4 pint) full-fat milk to scalding point in a small pan and add 1 tsp vanilla extract. Put 6 egg yolks into a bowl and pour over the hot milk, whisking. Pour back into the cleaned pan and cook over a low heat, stirring until the mixture coats the back of a spoon. Put 200g (7oz) small white marshmallows in a bowl, strain the warm custard over and stir until they have almost melted. Cool quickly, then cover and chill for 30 minutes. Fold 300ml (1/2 pint) lightly whipped double cream into the custard. Pour into a freezerproof container and freeze for 3–4 hours until just firm. (Alternatively, if you have an ice cream maker, churn the custard until just firm.) Stir in 125g (4oz) chopped chocolate and freeze.

1 Preheat the oven to 130°C (110°C fan oven) mark 1/2. Line two baking sheets with baking parchment. Using a felt-tip pen, mark out two 23cm (9in) diameter circles, then turn the paper over.

2 Sift the caster and muscovado sugars together. Whisk the egg whites in a clean, grease-free bowl until they're stiff and dry. Whisk in the sugars, 1 tbsp at a time, until the mixture is glossy and very stiff – about 5 minutes; then whisk in the cornflour and vinegar.

3 Spoon just over half the meringue on to one of the baking sheets in a garland shape and sprinkle with half the almonds, if using. Spread the remaining mixture evenly over the other circle to cover it completely. Sprinkle with the remaining almonds and bake for 2–2 1/2 hours, then turn off the oven and leave the meringues inside to cool for 30 minutes.

4 About 30 minutes before serving, remove the ice cream from the freezer to soften. Put the meringue circle on a serving plate. Slice the bananas and scatter evenly over the base.

5 Using a spoon or ice cream scoop, spoon the ice cream mixture over the bananas and put the meringue garland on top, pressing down gently. Decorate with chocolate shavings and a dusting of icing sugar, then serve immediately.

Serves	FOR THE CONFIDENT COOK		NUTRITIONAL INFORMATION	
10	**Preparation Time** 45 minutes, plus chilling, freezing and softening	**Cooking Time** 2 1/2 hours, plus cooling	**Per Serving** 479 calories, 24g fat (of which 14g saturates), 62g carbohydrate, 0.2g salt	Gluten free

Try Something Different

Blueberry Cheesecake: replace the raspberries with blueberries.
Pineapple and Ginger Cheesecake: omit the almonds and replace the almond biscuits with 250g (9oz) crushed gingernut biscuits. Omit the almond extract. Replace the raspberries with fresh pineapple chunks.

Raspberry Cheesecake

25g (1oz) blanched almonds, lightly toasted, then finely chopped

225g (8oz) almond butter biscuits, crushed

100g (3½oz) unsalted butter, melted

a few drops of almond extract

450g (1lb) raspberries

300g (11oz) Greek yogurt

150g (5oz) low-fat soft cheese

1 tbsp powdered gelatine

2 medium egg whites

50g (2oz) icing sugar

1 Grease a 20.5cm (8in) round springform cake tin. Mix the almonds with the crushed biscuits and melted butter. Add the almond extract. Spoon into the tin, then press down with the back of a spoon. Chill.

2 To make the filling, purée 225g (8oz) raspberries in a blender, then press through a sieve. Put three-quarters of the purée to one side and return the rest to the blender. Add the yogurt and cheese, then whiz to blend. Transfer to a bowl. Sprinkle the gelatine over 2 tbsp water in a heatproof bowl and leave to soak for 2–3 minutes. Put the bowl over a pan of simmering water until the gelatine has dissolved.

3 Whisk the egg whites with the icing sugar until thick and shiny. Fold into the cheese mixture. Arrange half the remaining berries over the biscuit base. Pour the cheese mixture over the berries. Add the reserved purée and swirl with a knife to marble. Top with the remaining berries and chill for 3–4 hours.

Serves	EASY		NUTRITIONAL INFORMATION
10	**Preparation Time** 25 minutes, plus chilling	**Cooking Time** 5 minutes	**Per Serving** 270 calories, 19g fat (of which 10g saturates), 20g carbohydrate, 0.5g salt

butter to grease
6 large eggs, separated
250g (9oz) golden caster sugar
150g (5oz) self-raising flour, sifted
150g (5oz) ground almonds
grated zest of 2 oranges and juice of 3 large oranges
100g (3½oz) golden granulated sugar
225ml (8fl oz) sweet white wine
350g (12oz) strawberries, thinly sliced

For the white chocolate ganache
225g (8oz) white chocolate, chopped
600ml (1 pint) double cream

Orange and White Chocolate Cake

1 Preheat the oven to 180°C (160°C fan oven) mark 4. Grease and line a 23cm (9in) round deep cake tin.

2 Put the egg whites in a clean, grease-free bowl and whisk until they form soft peaks. Gradually beat in 50g (2oz) caster sugar and whisk until the mixture is stiff and glossy. Put the egg yolks and remaining sugar in another bowl. Whisk until soft and moussey. Carefully stir in the flour, fold in a third of the egg whites, then fold in the remaining egg whites, ground almonds and orange zest. Pour the mixture into the prepared tin and bake for 35 minutes or until a skewer inserted into the centre comes out clean. Leave in the tin for 10 minutes, then turn out on to a wire rack to cool.

3 Put the orange juice, granulated sugar and wine in a small pan and stir over a low heat until the sugar has dissolved. Bring to the boil and bubble for 5 minutes or until syrupy. Cool and set aside.

4 To make the ganache, put the chocolate in a heatproof bowl with half the cream. Put the bowl over a pan of gently simmering water until the chocolate melts, then stir to combine. Cool, then beat with a wooden spoon until cold and thick. Whip the remaining cream lightly and beat a large spoonful into the chocolate cream to loosen it. Fold in the remainder. Chill for 2 hours.

5 Cut the cake in half horizontally, pierce all over with a skewer and put it, cut sides up, on a baking sheet. Spoon over the orange syrup and leave to soak in. Spread a quarter of the ganache over the base cake and scatter with 225g (8oz) strawberries. Cover with the top half of the cake and press down lightly. Using a palette knife, smooth the remaining ganache over the top and sides of the cake. Chill for up to 4 hours. Decorate with the remaining strawberries and serve.

FOR THE CONFIDENT COOK		NUTRITIONAL INFORMATION		Serves
Preparation Time 35 minutes, plus chilling	**Cooking Time** 40 minutes, plus cooling	**Per Serving** 544 calories, 35g fat (of which 18g saturates), 48g carbohydrate, 0.3g salt	Vegetarian	**14**

Cardamom and Mango Cake

50g (2oz) unsalted butter, plus extra to grease

4 green cardamom pods

a good pinch of saffron

4 large eggs

125g (4oz) caster sugar

100g (3½oz) plain flour

For the filling, mango sauce and decoration

150ml (¼ pint) double cream

150g (5oz) Greek yogurt

3 tbsp icing sugar, plus extra to dust

2 large ripe mangoes

4 tbsp orange juice

orange segments

1 Preheat the oven to 180°C (160°C fan oven) mark 4. Grease and baseline two 18cm (7in) sandwich tins, or one deep 18cm (7in) round cake tin.

2 Split the cardamom pods and remove the black seeds. Crush the seeds to a powder with the saffron strands. Put the butter into a pan and heat gently until melted, then remove from the heat and leave to cool for a few minutes until beginning to thicken.

3 Put the eggs and caster sugar into a large heatproof bowl and whisk until evenly blended, using an electric whisk. Put the bowl over a pan of hot water and whisk until pale and thick enough to leave a trail on the surface when the whisk is lifted. Remove the bowl from the pan and whisk until cool and thick.

4 Sift the spices and flour together. Fold half into the whisked mixture using a large metal spoon or plastic spatula. Pour the cooled butter around the edge of the mixture, leaving the sediment behind. Gradually fold it in very lightly, cutting through the mixture until it is all incorporated. Carefully fold in the remaining flour as lightly as possible. Pour into the prepared tins. Bake for 25–30 minutes, until well risen and the cakes spring back when lightly pressed. Run a small knife around the cake edge to loosen and leave in the tins for 5 minutes.

5 To make the filling, whip the cream until it holds its shape. Stir in the yogurt with 2 tbsp icing sugar. Sandwich the cake with the cream mixture and one sliced mango. Chill for 2–3 hours.

6 To make the sauce, liquidise the remaining mango flesh with 1 tbsp icing sugar and the orange juice; pass through a nylon sieve to remove all the fibres. Cover and chill. Just before serving, decorate the cake with orange segments and dust with icing sugar. Serve with the mango sauce.

A LITTLE EFFORT		NUTRITIONAL INFORMATION		Serves
Preparation Time 45 minutes	**Cooking Time** 25–30 minutes, plus cooling	**Per Serving** 274 calories, 16g fat (of which 9g saturates), 31g carbohydrate, 0.2g salt	Vegetarian	**10**

a little vegetable oil

6 medium eggs, separated

200g (7oz) caster sugar, plus extra to dust

2–3 drops vanilla extract

50g (2oz) cocoa powder, sifted

For the filling

125g (4oz) plain chocolate (at least 50% cocoa solids), broken into pieces

300ml (½ pint) double cream

225g (8oz) unsweetened chestnut purée

200ml (7fl oz) full-fat crème fraîche

50g (2oz) icing sugar

Chocolate and Chestnut Roulade

1 Preheat the oven to 180°C (160°C fan oven) mark 4. Lightly oil a 33 x 20.5cm (13 x 8in) Swiss roll tin, then line it with greaseproof paper.

2 Put the egg yolks into a large bowl. Add the caster sugar and vanilla extract, then whisk until pale and thick. Fold in the sifted cocoa powder using a large metal spoon. In a clean, grease-free bowl, whisk the egg whites until they form stiff peaks, then fold into the cocoa mixture. Spoon into the prepared tin, spread evenly and bake for 20–25 minutes until just cooked – the top should be springy to the touch.

3 Leave to cool in the tin for 10–15 minutes. Put a sheet of baking parchment on to the worksurface and dust with caster sugar. Carefully turn out the roulade on to the parchment, then leave to cool. Peel away the lining paper.

4 Meanwhile, make the filling. Melt the chocolate in a heatproof bowl over a pan of gently simmering water. In a separate bowl, lightly whip the cream. Beat the chestnut purée into the chocolate until smooth; the mixture will be quite thick. Whisk in the crème fraîche and icing sugar. Beat 1 tbsp of the whipped cream into the chocolate mixture, then use a metal spoon to fold in half the remaining cream.

5 Spread the filling over the roulade, then spread the remaining cream on top. Roll up the roulade, using the baking parchment to help you, and lift on to a serving plate. Dust with caster sugar.

Serves 10	EASY		NUTRITIONAL INFORMATION	
	Preparation Time 20 minutes	**Cooking Time** 20–25 minutes, plus cooling	**Per Serving** 409 calories, 28g fat (of which 17g saturates), 36g carbohydrate, 0.3g salt	Vegetarian • Gluten free

200g (7oz) unsalted butter, melted, plus extra to grease

250g (9oz) self-raising flour, sifted

100g (3½oz) golden caster sugar

4 medium eggs, beaten

125g (4oz) raspberries

2 large almost-ripe peaches or nectarines, halved, stoned and sliced

4 tbsp apricot jam

juice of ½ lemon

Raspberry and Peach Cake

1 Preheat the oven to 190°C (170°C fan oven) mark 5. Grease a 20.5cm (8in) springform cake tin and baseline with baking parchment.

2 Put the flour and sugar into a large bowl. Make a well in the centre, and add the melted butter and the eggs. Mix well.

3 Spread half the mixture over the base of the cake tin and add half the raspberries and sliced peaches or nectarines. Spoon on the remaining cake mixture, smooth over, then add the remaining raspberries and peaches or nectarines, pressing them down into the mixture slightly.

4 Bake for 1–1¼ hours until risen and golden, and a skewer inserted into the centre comes out clean. Remove from the oven and leave in the tin to cool for 10 minutes.

5 Warm the jam and the lemon juice together in a small pan and brush over the cake to glaze.

EASY		NUTRITIONAL INFORMATION		Serves
Preparation Time 15 minutes	**Cooking Time** 1–1¼ hours, plus cooling	**Per Serving** 405 calories, 24g fat (of which 14g saturates), 44g carbohydrate, 0.8g salt	Vegetarian	**8**

Cook's Tips

For fresh coconut slices, use a vegetable peeler to pare thin slices, sprinkle with a little caster sugar and grill until lightly browned.

To make ahead Complete the recipe to the end of step 3. Wrap well in clingfilm and greaseproof paper and store in a cool place for two to three days.

To use Complete the recipe.

Tropical Fruit Cake

125g (4oz) unsalted butter, softened

200g (7oz) caster sugar

grated zest of 1 orange and 3 tbsp juice

2 large eggs, lightly beaten

a pinch of salt

125g (4oz) each semolina and desiccated coconut

200g (7oz) ground almonds

1 tsp baking powder

300ml (½ pint) double cream

icing sugar and vanilla extract to taste

1 mango, 1 papaya or pineapple, 1 star fruit and 1 banana, peeled and sliced

6 lychees, peeled and stones removed

50g (2oz) coconut slices (see Cook's Tips)

For the citrus syrup

pared zest of 1 orange and juice of 2 oranges

pared zest of 1 lemon and juice of 3 lemons

125g (4oz) caster sugar

1   Preheat the oven to 170°C (150°C fan oven) mark 3. Grease and baseline a 23cm (9in) springform cake tin. To make the cake, whisk together the butter and 125g (4oz) caster sugar in a food processor (or with an electric whisk) until pale and fluffy. Beat together the orange zest, eggs and salt, then beat into the butter mixture, a spoonful at a time. With a spatula or large metal spoon, fold in the semolina, desiccated coconut, ground almonds, baking powder and orange juice. Spoon the mixture into the prepared tin. Bake for 45–50 minutes until a skewer inserted into the centre comes out clean. Leave in the tin for 15 minutes, then turn out on to a wire rack to cool completely.

2   Meanwhile, make the citrus syrup. Put the orange and lemon zest and juice, caster sugar and 450ml (¾ pint) water in a pan. Bring to the boil and bubble for 15–20 minutes until syrupy. Set aside to cool.

3   Cut about 1cm (½ in) from the centre of the cake, crumble and keep the crumbs to one side. Prick the cake with a fine skewer – without piercing right through, or the syrup will run through – and spoon the syrup over. Set aside 3 tbsp of the syrup.

4   Whisk the cream to soft peaks, add the icing sugar and vanilla extract to taste. Carefully fold in the reserved cake crumbs, a third of the prepared fruit and the reserved syrup. Stir gently to combine, taking care not to mash the fruit. Spoon on to the cake.

5   Decorate with the remaining fruit and coconut slices. For the topping, put the remaining 75g (3oz) caster sugar in a pan and add 50ml (2fl oz) water, bring to the boil and bubble until the caramel turns a light brown. Carefully add 2 tbsp cold water. Drizzle over the cake while still warm and serve immediately.

Serves 8	FOR THE CONFIDENT COOK		NUTRITIONAL INFORMATION	
	Preparation Time 40 minutes	**Cooking Time** 1 hour 20 minutes, plus cooling	**Per Serving** 857 calories, 60g fat (of which 32g saturates), 74g carbohydrate, 0.3g salt	Vegetarian

Cook's Tip

Toffee Sauce: put 300g (11oz) light muscovado sugar, 300ml (½ pint) double cream and 50g (2oz) unsalted butter into a small heavy-based pan. Heat gently to dissolve the sugar, then simmer and stir for 3 minutes to thicken slightly. Pour into a jug.

Sweet Pumpkin Cake with Toffee Sauce

550g (1¼lb) pumpkin or butternut squash, cut into wedges

butter to grease

225g (8oz) self-raising flour, plus extra to dust

250ml (9fl oz) sunflower oil

275g (10oz) light muscovado sugar, plus extra to sprinkle

3 large eggs

1 tsp bicarbonate of soda

2 tsp ground ginger

1 tsp ground cinnamon

1 tsp nutmeg

a pinch of ground cloves

a pinch of ground allspice

Toffee Sauce (see Cook's Tip) to serve

1 Preheat the oven to 200°C (180°C fan oven) mark 6. Grease a 23cm (9in) kugelhopf tin generously with butter and dust with flour. Put the pumpkin on a baking sheet and roast for 40 minutes or until tender. Leave to cool for 15 minutes.

2 Reduce the oven temperature to 180°C (160°C fan oven) mark 4. Spoon out 250g (9oz) pumpkin flesh, put in a blender and whiz to a purée.

3 Put the oil and sugar in a freestanding mixer and whisk for 2 minutes (or use an electric whisk), then whisk in the eggs one at a time. Sift over the flour, bicarbonate of soda and spices, and fold in. Add the pumpkin purée and stir in gently.

4 Pour into the prepared tin. Bake for 40–45 minutes until risen, springy and shrinking from the edges. Leave in the tin for 10 minutes, then turn out and cool on a wire rack. To serve, drizzle the toffee sauce over the cake and sprinkle with muscovado sugar.

Serves 16	EASY		NUTRITIONAL INFORMATION	
	Preparation Time 25 minutes	**Cooking Time** 1½ hours, plus cooling	**Per Serving** 440 calories, 24g fat (of which 9g saturates), 55g carbohydrate, 0.3g salt	Vegetarian

40g (1½oz) unsalted butter, plus extra to grease
75g (3oz) plain flour, plus extra to dust
75g (3oz) golden caster sugar, plus extra to dust
3 large eggs
1 tbsp cornflour

To assemble
300ml (½ pint) double cream, lightly whipped
350g (12oz) fresh summer berries
icing sugar, to dust

Genoese Sponge

1. Preheat the oven to 180°C (160°C fan oven) mark 4. Grease and baseline two 18cm (7in) sandwich tins, or one deep 18cm (7in) round cake tin, then dust with a little flour and caster sugar.

2. Put the butter into a pan and heat gently until melted, then remove from the heat and leave to cool slightly for a few minutes until beginning to thicken.

3. Put the eggs and caster sugar into a large heatproof bowl and whisk until evenly blended, using an electric whisk. Put the bowl over a pan of hot water and whisk until pale and thick enough to leave a trail when the whisk is lifted. Remove the bowl from the pan and continue whisking until cool and thick.

4. Sift the flour and cornflour together. Fold half into the whisked mixture with a large metal spoon. Pour the cooled butter around the edge of the mixture, leaving the sediment behind. Gradually fold it in very lightly, cutting through the mixture until it is all incorporated. Carefully fold in the remaining flour as lightly as possible. Pour into the prepared tin(s).

5. Bake for 20–25 minutes, or the deep cake for 35–40 minutes, until well risen and the sponge springs back when lightly pressed. Loosen the cake edge and leave in the tins for 5 minutes. Turn out on to a wire rack, remove the lining paper and leave to cool. Mix together the cream and fruit and use to sandwich the cake together. Dust with icing sugar.

Try Something Different

Coffee Sponge: dissolve 1 tbsp espresso coffee powder in 2 tsp boiling water, mix with the melted butter and fold in at step 4. Fill with coffee mascarpone: dissolve 1 tbsp espresso coffee powder in 1 tbsp boiling water, then beat with 250g (9oz) mascarpone and 125g (4oz) sifted icing sugar until smooth.

EASY		NUTRITIONAL INFORMATION		Serves
Preparation Time 25 minutes	**Cooking Time** 20–40 minutes, plus cooling	**Per Serving** 433 calories, 34g fat (of which 20g saturates), 28g carbohydrate, 0.2g salt	Vegetarian	**6**

Cook's Tips

We used bottled lemon juice, as it gives a more intense lemony flavour than fresh juice.

The weight of the fruit may make it sink towards the bottom of the cake. Don't worry if this happens – it will still taste just as wonderful.

Other summer berries such as blackberries, loganberries and blackcurrants can be used if you like.

Lemon and Berry Crunch Cake

150g (5oz) unsalted butter, softened, plus extra to grease

2 medium eggs, plus 1 egg yolk

a pinch of salt

150g (5oz) caster sugar

150g (5oz) self-raising flour, sifted

grated zest and juice of 1 lemon

125g (4oz) raspberries and blueberries

For the lemon crunch topping

25ml (1fl oz) bottled lemon juice (see Cook's Tips)

225g (8oz) caster sugar

25g (1oz) rough white sugar cubes, lightly crushed

white currants, blackcurrants, wild strawberries and crème fraîche or Greek yogurt to serve

1 Preheat the oven to 170°C (150°C fan oven) mark 3. Grease and baseline a 1.1 litre (2 pint) loaf tin.

2 Lightly beat the eggs and egg yolk with the salt. Put the butter and sugar in a bowl, and beat until light and fluffy. Gradually beat in the eggs, beating for about 10 minutes.

3 Fold in the flour with the lemon zest and 2 tbsp of the juice (put the rest to one side). Fold in the raspberries and blueberries. Spoon the mixture into the prepared tin and bake for 50 minutes–1 hour. Leave in the tin for 5 minutes, then turn out on to a wire rack to cool.

4 To make the topping, mix together the reserved fresh lemon juice, bottled lemon juice and caster sugar. Spoon over the cake and sprinkle the top with crushed sugar. Set aside for 1 hour. Slice and serve with berries and crème fraîche or yogurt.

Serves 8	EASY		NUTRITIONAL INFORMATION	
	Preparation Time 40 minutes, plus setting	**Cooking Time** 1 hour, plus cooling	**Per Serving** 428 calories, 18g fat (of which 10g saturates), 67g carbohydrate, 0.5g salt	Vegetarian

Glossary

Baking blind Pre-baking a pastry case before filling. The pastry case is lined with greaseproof paper and weighted down with dried beans or ceramic baking beans.

Baking powder A raising agent consisting of an acid, usually cream of tartar and an alkali, such as bicarbonate of soda, which react to produce carbon dioxide. This expands during baking and makes cakes and breads rise.

Beat To incorporate air into an ingredient or mixture by agitating it vigorously with a spoon, fork, whisk or electric mixer. The technique is also used to soften ingredients.

Bind To mix beaten egg or other liquid into a dry mixture to hold it together.

Blanch To immerse food briefly in fast-boiling water to loosen skins, such as peaches or tomatoes, or to remove bitterness, or to destroy enzymes and preserve the colour, flavour and texture of vegetables (especially prior to freezing)

Brûlée A French term, literally meaning 'burnt', used to refer to a dish with a crisp coating of caramelised sugar.

Candying Method of preserving fruit or peel by impregnating with sugar.

Caramelise To heat sugar or sugar syrup slowly until it is brown in colour; ie forms a caramel

Chill To cool food in the fridge.

Compote Fresh or dried fruit stewed in sugar syrup. Served hot or cold.

Consistency Term used to describe the texture of a mixture, eg firm, dropping or soft.

Coulis A smooth fruit or vegetable purée, thinned if necessary to a pouring consistency.

Cream To beat together fat and sugar until the mixture is pale and fluffy, and resembles whipped cream in texture and colour. The method is used in cakes and puddings which contain a high proportion of fat and require the incorporation of a lot of air.

Crimp To decorate the edge of a pie, tart or shortbread by pinching it at regular intervals to give a fluted effect.

Curdle To cause sauces or creamed mixtures to separate, usually by overheating or over-beating.

Dice To cut food into small cubes.

Dredge To sprinkle food generously with flour, sugar, icing sugar etc.

Dust To sprinkle lightly with flour, cornflour, icing sugar etc.

Extract Concentrated flavouring, which is used in small quantities, eg yeast extract, vanilla extract.

Ferment Chemical change deliberately or accidentally brought about by fermenting agents, such as yeast or bacteria. Fermentation is utilised for making bread, yogurt, beer and wine.

Folding in Method of combining a whisked or creamed mixture with other ingredients by cutting and folding so that it retains its lightness. A large metal spoon or plastic-bladed spatula is used.

Frosting To coat leaves and flowers with a fine layer of sugar to use as a decoration. Also an American term for icing cakes.

Fry To cook food in hot fat or oil. There are various methods: shallow-frying in a little fat in a shallow pan; deep-frying where the food is totally immersed in oil; dry-frying in which fatty foods are cooked in a non-stick pan without extra fat.

Galette Cooked savoury or sweet mixture shaped into a round.

Garnish A decoration, usually edible, such as lemon, which is used to enhance the appearance of a dish.

Glaze A glossy coating given to sweet and savoury dishes to improve their appearance and sometimes flavour. Ingredients for glazes include beaten egg, egg white, milk and syrup.

Gluten A protein constituent of grains, such as wheat and rye, which develops when the flour is mixed with water to give the dough elasticity.

Griddle A flat, heavy, metal plate used on the hob for cooking scones or for searing savoury ingredients.

Grind To reduce foods such as coffee beans, nuts and whole spices to small particles using a food mill, pestle and mortar, electric grinder or food processor.

Hull To remove the stalk and calyx from soft fruits, such as strawberries.

Infuse To immerse flavourings, such as aromatic vegetables, herbs, spices and vanilla, in a liquid to impart flavour. Usually the infused liquid is brought to the boil, then left to stand for a while.

Julienne Fine 'matchstick' strips of citrus zest or vegetables, sometimes used as a decoration or garnish.

Knead To work dough by pummelling with the heel of the hand.

Knock back To knead a yeast dough for a second time after rising, to ensure an even texture.

Macerate To soften and flavour raw or dried foods by soaking in a liquid, eg soaking fruit in alcohol.

Parboil To boil a vegetable or other food for part of its cooking time before finishing it by another method.

Pare To finely peel the skin or zest from vegetables or fruit.

Patty tin Tray of cup-shaped moulds for cooking small cakes and deep tartlets. Also called a bun tin.

Poach To cook food gently in liquid at simmering point; the surface should be just trembling.

Prove To leave bread dough to rise (usually for a second time) after shaping.

Purée To pound, sieve or liquidise vegetables, fish or fruit to a smooth pulp. Purées often form the basis for soups and sauces.

Reduce To fast-boil stock or other liquid in an uncovered pan to evaporate water and concentrate the flavour.

Roast To cook food by dry heat in the oven.

Roulade Soufflé or sponge mixture rolled around a savoury or sweet filling.

Roux A mixture of equal quantities of butter (or other fat) and flour cooked together to form the basis of many sauces.

Rubbing in Method of incorporating fat into flour by rubbing between the fingertips, used when a short texture is required. Used for pastry, cakes, scones and biscuits.

Scald To pour boiling water over food to clean it, or loosen skin, eg tomatoes. Also used to describe heating milk to just below boiling point.

Score To cut parallel lines in the surface of food, such as fish (or the fat layer on meat), to improve its appearance or help it cook more quickly.

Shred To grate cheese or slice vegetables into very fine pieces or strips.

Sieve To press food through a perforated sieve to obtain a smooth texture.

Sift To shake dry ingredients through a sieve to remove lumps.

Simmer To keep a liquid just below boiling point.

Skim To remove froth, scum or fat from the surface of stock, gravy, stews, jam etc. Use either a skimmer, a spoon or kitchen paper.

Steep To immerse food in warm or cold liquid to soften it, and sometimes to draw out strong flavours.

Stew To cook food, such as fruit and tougher cuts of meat, in flavoured liquid which is kept at simmering point.

Tepid The term used to describe a temperature of approximately blood heat, ie 37°C (98.7°F).

Vanilla sugar Sugar in which a vanilla pod has been stored to impart its flavour.

Whipping (whisking) Beating air rapidly into a mixture either with a manual or electric whisk. Whipping usually refers to cream.

Zest The thin, coloured outer layer of citrus fruit, which can be removed in fine strips with a zester.

Index